QUiLTER's favorites

A Collection of **19 Radiant Projects** for All Skill Levels

EDITORS' PICK **VOL. 2**

Pieced Points & Stars

C&T PUBLISHING

Text and artwork copyright © 2009 by C&T Publishing, Inc.

Publisher: Amy Marson

Creative Director: Gailen Runge

Acquisitions Editor:
Susanne Woods

Editor: Liz Aneloski

Technical Editor: Carolyn Aune

Proofreader: Wordfirm Inc.

Cover/Book Designer:
Kerry Graham

Design Director: Kristy Zacharias

Production Coordinator:
Kirstie L. Pettersen

Production Editor: Julia Cianci

Illustrator: C&T Publishing

Photography by C&T Publishing, Inc., unless otherwise noted.

Published by C&T Publishing, Inc., P.O. Box 1456, Lafayette, CA 94549

Library of Congress Cataloging-in-Publication Data

Quilter's favorites--pieced points & stars : a collection of 19 radiant projects for all skill levels.

   p. cm.

ISBN 978-1-57120-836-1 (softcover)

1. Patchwork--Patterns. 2. Quilting--Patterns. I. C&T Publishing.

TT835.Q4877 2010

746.46'041--dc22

                    2009023377

Printed in China

10 9 8 7 6 5 4 3 2 1

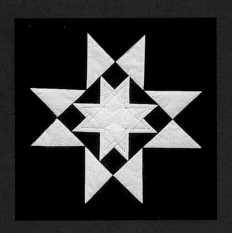

The Editors of C&T Publishing are proud to present our second collection of *Quilter's Favorites.*

For this collection we've gathered 19 quilt projects that include points or stars. They range from super simple half-square triangles to more challenging paper-pieced New York Beauty blocks—and everything in between. There's something for every quilter's style. So take a look at the projects, choose the ones that are just right for you, and get started making your own unique versions with the inspiration and instructions you can always count on in books from C&T Publishing.

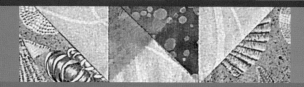

CONTENTS

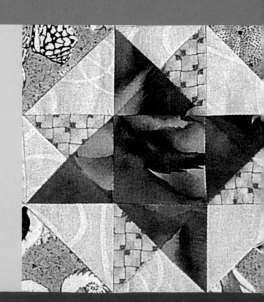

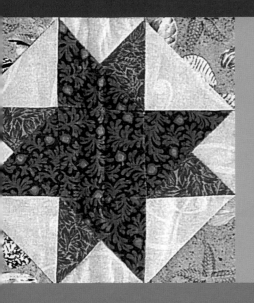

half-square triangle quilt

beginner

Finished half-square triangle size: 5″

Half-Square Triangle Quilt, 59½″ × 64½″, made by Alex Anderson and machine quilted by Paula Reid

Bright fabrics are always fun to work with. The coordinating fabrics I picked were dictated by all the different froggie colors in my focus fabric.

Half-Square Triangles

The half-square triangle has two edges that are on the straight of grain. The long edge is on the bias. You must handle the pieces carefully because until they are sewn into squares the triangle can stretch and distort from the long bias edge.

Half-square triangle

Cutting a Half-Square Triangle

- Never press the fabric shape once it has been cut and before it has been sewn.

- Never pull the units through the sewing machine as you stitch them together, since this can stretch the shapes. Let your machine do the work for you.

Materials

Yardage is based on 42″-wide fabric.

Light fabrics: ¼ yard each of 8 or 9 different fabrics

Dark fabrics: ¼ yard each of 8 or 9 different fabrics

Stripe: ½ yard for inner border

Focus fabric: 1¾ yards for outer border and some of the half-square triangles (choose this fabric first)

Binding: ½ yard

Backing: 4 yards

Batting: 70″ × 75″

Half-square triangle unit

Cutting

Lights: Cut 45 squares 5⅞″ × 5⅞″, then cut in half diagonally from corner to corner.

Darks: Cut 45 squares 5⅞″ × 5⅞″, then cut in half diagonally from corner to corner.

Making the Blocks

Use a ¼″ seam allowance. The arrows show which way to press the seam allowances.

1. Put the light triangles in 1 pile and the dark triangles in another pile. Randomly pick 1 light triangle and 1 dark triangle from the piles.

2. Place the two triangles right sides together, carefully matching the edges. Sew along the long diagonal edge.

3. Do not cut the threads to remove the first set. Repeat Steps 1 and 2.

4. Feed the second set into the sewing machine right after the first set. This is called chain piecing.

5. Repeat Steps 1, 2, and 3 to make 90 half-square triangle units.

6. Cut the threads that hold the units together. Press the seam toward the dark fabric on each

Chain piecing

pair of triangles. Trim off the bunny ears. These are the small triangles of fabric that extend over the edge.

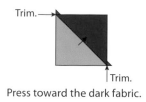

Trim. ⟶

Trim.

Press toward the dark fabric.

Putting the Quilt Top Together

1. Lay out the blocks as shown. Note that they are in a straight set.

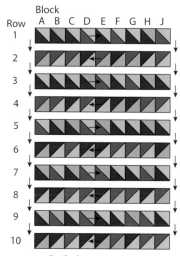

Quilt Construction

You will sew the blocks into rows and then you will sew the rows together.

2. Place block B on top of block A, right sides together. Pin the edge where they should join. Sew the seam. Press the seam following the arrows for each row. Lay this pair back in the quilt layout.

3. Place block C on top of block B, right sides together. Pin, sew, and press as you did before.

4. Repeat for the remaining blocks in the row.

5. Repeat for the blocks in each row.

6. Place row 1 on top of row 2, right sides together, and carefully pin the top edge, matching the seams. Sew the seam.

7. Place row 3 on top of row 2, right sides together, and pin the bottom edge. Sew as you did before.

8. Repeat for the remaining rows. Press.

Your quilt top should measure 45½″ × 50½″. If it does, use the instructions below to cut and attach the inner and outer border strips. If it doesn't, see page 105 to measure and cut the correct border lengths for your quilt top.

INNER BORDER

1. Cut 6 strips 2″ × the fabric width. Trim off the selvages. Sew these strips together to form 1 long strip.

2. Cut 2 strips 50½″ long.

3. Sew on the side inner border strips. Press.

4. Cut 2 strips 48½″ long from the long pieced strip.

5. Sew on the top and bottom inner border strips. Press.

OUTER BORDER

1. Cut 6 strips 6″ × the fabric width. Trim off the selvages. Sew these strips together to form 1 long strip.

2. Cut 2 strips 53½″ long.

3. Sew on the side outer border strips. Press.

4. Cut 2 strips 59½″ long from the long pieced strip.

5. Sew on the top and bottom outer border strips. Press.

Quilting and Finishing

Refer to pages 106–108 for quilting and finishing instructions.

1. Layer and baste the quilt. Quilt by hand or machine.

2. Finish the quilt.

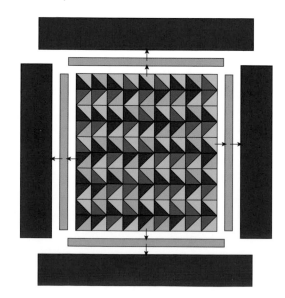

in the limelight

beginner

Finished block size: 7½″ × 7½″

In the Limelight, 33¼″ × 40¾″, made by M'Liss Rae Hawley and machine quilted by Barbara Dau

I do a great deal of my sewing at night and enjoy taking a break now and then to look at the stars. I see them as sparks of color glittering in the inky black sky.

To capture this look in my quilt, I chose a single black batik for the block backgrounds and a variety of chartreuse batiks—suggested by the border fabric, which I planned to use all along—for star centers. Beyond that, my choices were much more random: I just selected two different, colorful batiks for the star points in each block. I added couching in the border to suggest star trails, a detail that worked well to tie the quilt together, both creatively and thematically.

This is a wonderful quilt for a beginner. Although the blocks are set side by side, none of the points touch, which is unusual for a star block! For this reason, it also makes a great choice for a group quilt, where slight variations in block size can sometimes be a problem.

Materials

Yardage is based on 42″-wide fabric.

⅔ yard of fabric for block background (A and C)

One 2″ × 2″ square each of 12 assorted prints for star centers (D)

Two 3⅞″ × 3⅞″ squares each of 12 assorted prints for star points (B)

One 4¼″ × 4¼″ square each of 12 assorted prints for star points (E)

¼ yard of fabric for inner border

1⅜ yards of fabric for outer border and binding

1½ yards of fabric for backing

⅜ yard of fabric for hanging sleeve

41″ × 49″ piece of batting

Assorted decorative threads, ribbons, and yarns for couching

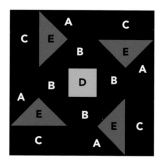

Block diagram

Cutting

Cut strips on the crosswise grain (from selvage to selvage) unless otherwise noted.

From the assorted star point prints:

Cut each 4¼″ square in half twice diagonally to make 4 quarter-square triangles (48 total) (E).

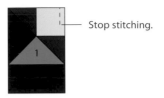

From the assorted star point prints:

Cut each 3⅞″ square in half once diagonally to make 2 half-square triangles (48 total) (B).

From the background fabric:

Cut 2 strips, 4¼″ × 40″. Crosscut into 12 squares, 4¼″ × 4¼″. Cut each square in half twice diagonally to make 4 quarter-square triangles (48 total) (A).

Cut 5 strips, 2″ × 40″. Crosscut into 48 rectangles, 2″ × 3½″ (C).

From the inner-border fabric:

Cut 4 strips, ⅞″ × 40″.

From the lengthwise grain of the outer-border and binding fabric:

Cut 4 strips, 5″ × 46″.

Cut 4 strips, 3″ × 46″.

From the hanging-sleeve fabric:

Cut 1 strip, 8½″ × 40″.

Making the Blocks

1. With right sides together, sew one print quarter-square triangle (E) to one background quarter-square triangle (A) along one short edge, as shown. Press. Make 48 in matching sets of 4.

Make 48.

2. With right sides together, sew one print half-square triangle (B) to each unit from Step 1, as shown. Press. Make 48 in matching sets of 4.

Make 48.

3. With right sides together, sew one 2″ × 3½″ background rectangle (C) to each unit from Step 2, as shown. Press. Make 48.

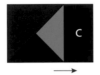

Make 48.

4. Arrange one 2″ star center square and 4 matching units from Step 3, labeling the units as shown.

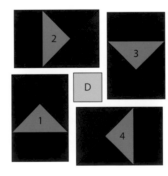

5. With right sides together, sew the star center square to the upper-right edge of Unit 1, stopping approximately halfway with a backstitch to

make a partial seam. Finger-press the seam away from the square.

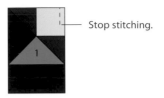

Stop stitching.

6. Sew the remaining units around the star center square in the order shown, rotating the block as you sew each seam. Press the seams away from the square.

Stitch complete seam.

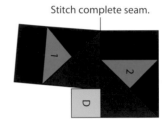

Stitch complete seam.

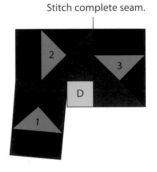

Move Unit 1 out of the way and stitch complete seam.

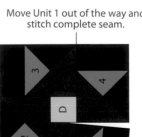

7. Finish sewing the seam between Unit 1 and the center square/Unit 4. Press the seam away from the square.

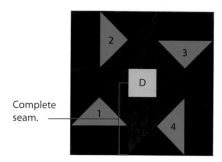

Complete seam.

8. Repeat Steps 4–7 to complete 12 Shooting Star blocks.

fussy cut for fun!

If your quilt is built around a specific theme, you might like to choose a fabric (or fabrics) with motifs you can fussy cut for the star centers (piece D), as Annette Barca did for her quilt *Happy Dog Days with Matilda*, in honor of Adrienne's beloved dachshund.

Detail of a Shooting Star block with fussy-cut center from a quilt by Annette Barca.

Putting the Quilt Top Together

1. Arrange the blocks in 4 horizontal rows of 3 blocks each, as shown in the assembly diagram.

2. Sew the blocks together into rows. Press. Sew the rows together. Press.

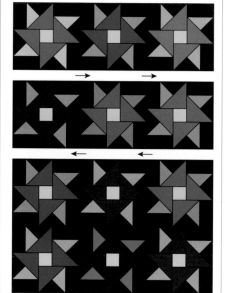

Assembly diagram

3. Refer to the Couching instructions on right to couch a variety of decorative threads, ribbons, and yarns onto each 5″-wide outer-border strip.

4. Fold each ⅞″-wide inner-border strip in half lengthwise to find and mark its midpoint. Repeat with each embellished 5″-wide outer-border strip. With right sides together, midpoints matched, and long raw edges aligned, sew the inner-border strips to the embellished outer-

border strips in pairs, as shown. Press. Make 4.

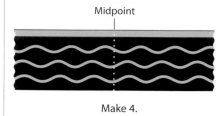

Midpoint

Make 4.

5. Refer to Mitered Corners Borders (pages 104–105) to measure, fit, and sew the border units to the quilt. Miter the corners. Press the seams toward the border units.

Quilting and Finishing

Refer to pages 106–108 for quilting and finishing instructions.

1. Layer and baste the quilt. Quilt by hand or machine.

2. Finish the quilt.

Couching

I love to add couching to my quilts. It creates visual interest and texture, while at the same time allowing me to enhance the theme of my quilt with an additional layer of creativity.

Couching is an embellishment technique that involves using decorative topstitching to attach a variety of decorative threads, yarns, or ribbons to the surface of a quilt. Here are some tips for a creative—and successful—couching experience:

■ Experiment first! Select a variety of trims and threads that complement your fabric choices and quilt theme. The more you have to choose from, the better! Couch the threads and trims to a sample of the intended background fabric, using a variety of stitches in both matching and contrasting threads. This allows you to discover what works best for your quilt and which foot works best for each trim and stitch. Document your findings for easy reference.

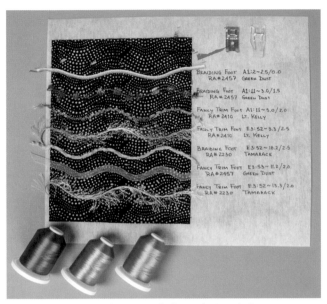

My couching sample for *In the Limelight*

■ Cut the outer border as instructed. Then cut a strip of tear-away stabilizer 1″ wider than the border width × the border length. Use a spray adhesive or pins to secure the stabilizer to the wrong side of the border strip.

■ Allowing for a ¼″ seam allowance, use a chalk marker to draw three serpentine (curvy) lines on the right side of the stabilized border strip. Space the lines somewhat evenly, but don't worry about the corners. As you see in the quilt photo on page 9 and in the corner detail below, they don't need to match to look good.

■ Referring to your couching sample and working one line at a time, place your selected yarns and threads over the marked lines and stitch the trims in place. Remove the stabilizer and sew the borders to the quilt as instructed.

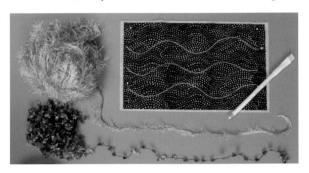

Detail of couching on *In the Limelight*: I used three different trims on each side of my quilt and stitched them in place with color-matched thread.

pyramid color play

Advanced Beginner

Finished block size: 5″

Pyramid Color Play, 50″ x 70″, made by Cheryl Malkowski

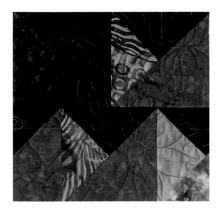

Here is a great quilt to show off your sense of color. There are 14 block colorations and you can have fun blending one block into the next. As you select fabric, think about the order of the color wheel. If you have a hard time choosing all the colors at once, just start by making the A blocks; lay them out and then choose the fabrics for the B blocks. Go on to the next block after you finish the previous one.

Fabric Requirements

Yardage is based on 42″-wide fabric unless noted.	

Blues and greens make up the most blocks, so keep that in mind as you choose your color combinations. Select 14 light fat quarters, paired with 14 related dark fat quarters. Of the 3 color combinations you want to use the most in the quilt, buy 1 extra fat quarter of each dark.

Fabric	Amount
Light colors for Position 1	Think color wheel! 14 fat quarters
Black for Position 2	1½ yards
Dark colors for Position 3	Pair these up with light Position 1 fabrics. 17 fat quarters
Black (for binding)	½ yard
Batting	54″ × 74″
108″-wide backing	1⅝ yards

Cutting and Block Construction

Sketch numbered blocks and glue small pieces of fabric to them to remind you of your color placement.

Follow the directions for making Y Blocks on pages 99–101.

			# Position 1, cut 6½″ × 6½″ light color	# Position 2, cut 6½″ × 6½″ black (37 total squares needed)	# Position 3, cut 6″ × 6″ dark color	Total to make of each block
Block A			1	1	2	4
Block B			2	2	4	8
Block C			2	2	4	8
Block D			2	2	4	8
Block E			3	3	6	12
Block F			3	3	6	12
Block G			4	4	8	16
Block H			5	5	10	20
Block I			3	3	6	12
Block J			4	4	8	16
Block K			3	3	6	12
Block L			2	2	4	8
Block M			1	1	2	4
Block N			2	2	4	7

Quilt Assembly

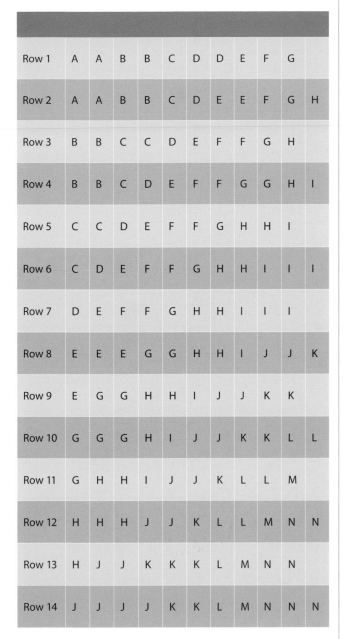

Row 1	A	A	B	B	C	D	D	E	F	G	
Row 2	A	A	B	B	C	D	E	E	F	G	H
Row 3	B	B	C	C	D	E	F	F	G	H	
Row 4	B	B	C	D	E	F	F	G	G	H	I
Row 5	C	C	D	E	F	F	G	H	H	I	
Row 6	C	D	E	F	F	G	H	H	I	I	I
Row 7	D	E	F	F	G	H	H	I	I	I	
Row 8	E	E	E	G	H	H	I	J	J	K	
Row 9	E	G	G	H	H	I	J	J	K	K	
Row 10	G	G	G	H	I	J	J	K	K	L	L
Row 11	G	H	H	I	J	J	K	L	L	M	
Row 12	H	H	H	J	J	K	L	L	M	N	N
Row 13	H	J	J	K	K	K	L	M	N	N	
Row 14	J	J	J	J	K	K	L	M	N	N	N

Putting the Quilt Top Together

1. Using the Quilt Assembly chart, diagram, and project photo as guides, place the blocks according to your own vision for the quilt. The project quilt is arranged according to the color wheel.

Note that all the even-numbered rows have 11 blocks, 1 block more than the odd-numbered rows. Cut off 2½˝ from each end of the even-numbered rows.

2½˝   2½˝

Trim 2½˝ from each end of the even-numbered rows.

2. Stitch the horizontal rows together and press the seam allowances to one side. Then stitch the rows together to complete the quilt center. Press.

Quilting and Finishing

Refer to pages 106–108 for quilting and finishing instructions.

1. Layer and baste the quilt. Quilt by hand or machine.

2. Finish the quilt.

Quilt assembly

sun and sea

advanced beginner

Finished block size: 5˝

Sun and Sea, 45˝ x 55˝, made by Linda Jenkins, Becky Goldsmith, and Elsie Ridgley; and machine quilted by Mary Covey

This scrappy mix of blues with many shades of orange sparkles like sunshine on ocean water. Blue and orange are complementary colors—they are opposite each other on the color wheel. Complementary colors play well together and provide maximum color contrast.

The pinwheel design itself can be hard to spot. Instead, your eyes keep moving, finding all sorts of patterns among the triangles.

In the borders, placing the dark edge of each triangle-square against the outside of the quilt prevents your eye from moving off the quilt. The points point back into the center, directing you to go back for another look.

Materials

Yardage is based on 42″-wide fabric.

Light fabric(s) for triangle-squares: 2⅓ yards OR ⅛ yard each of 26 different fabrics

Dark fabric(s) for triangle-squares: 2⅓ yards OR ⅛ yard each of 26 different fabrics

Inner border: ½ yard

Binding: ⅞ yard

Backing and sleeve: 3½ yards

Batting: 49″ × 59″

Cutting

Light fabric(s)

Triangle-squares: Cut 26 strips 3″ × 40″; then cut 328 squares 3″ × 3″.

Dark fabric(s)

Triangle-squares: Cut 26 strips 3″ × 40″; then cut 328 squares 3″ × 3″.

Inner border fabric

Cut 5 strips 3″ × 40″.

Binding fabric

Refer to pages 107–108 for making continuous bias.

Cut 1 square 24″ × 24″ to make a 2½″-wide continuous bias strip at least 215″ long.

Making the Blocks

1. Draw a diagonal line on the wrong side of each light 3″ × 3″ square.

2. Place a light and a dark square right sides together. Sew them together on the diagonal. Repeat for all squares. This is a good opportunity to chain together the squares.

3. Trim away the excess fabric, leaving a ¼″ seam allowance.

4. Press the seam allowances toward the dark side of the triangle-square.

5. Set aside 76 triangle-squares for the pieced outer border.

6. Place the top 2 triangle-squares in each Pinwheel block right sides together. Let the diagonal seams nest together. Pin and then sew the squares together. Press the seam allowance toward the light triangle.

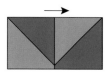

7. Sew and press the bottom 2 triangle-squares together in the same manner.

8. Place the 2 halves of each block right sides together on the table. Use a positioning pin to match the center points. Pin and then sew the blocks together.

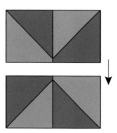

9. Press the seam allowances in each block in one direction. The seam allowances in neighboring blocks should be pressed in alternate directions so they nest together. Your Pinwheel blocks should now measure 5½″ × 5½″.

Inner Border

The inner border must be cut to the size specified because the outer border is pieced.

1. Cut off the selvages from both ends of the inner border strips.

2. Sew the strips end to end, right sides together. Press the seam allowances in one direction.

3. Cut 2 strips 3″ × 45½″ for the side inner borders.

4. Cut 2 strips 3″ × 40½″ for the top and bottom inner borders.

Putting the Quilt Top Together

Refer to the quilt assembly diagram for quilt construction.

1. Put all of the blocks and border strips on your design wall. Doing so helps you keep the blocks oriented correctly.

2. Sew 7 Pinwheel blocks together into a row. Make 9 rows. Press the seam allowances in alternate directions from row to row.

3. Sew the rows together. Press the seams toward the bottom.

4. Sew the side inner borders to the quilt. Press the seam allowances toward the border.

5. Sew the top and bottom inner borders to the quilt. Press the seam allowances toward the border.

6. Sew 20 triangle-squares together for each side outer border. Pay attention to the orientation of the triangle-squares. Press the seam allowances toward the light fabrics.

7. Sew the side outer borders to the quilt. Press the seam allowances toward the inner border.

8. Sew 18 triangle-squares together for the top and bottom outer borders. Pay attention to the orientation of the triangle-squares. Press the seam allowances toward the light fabrics.

9. Sew the top and bottom outer borders to the quilt. Press the seam allowances toward the inner border.

Quilting and Finishing

Refer to pages 106–108 for quilting and finishing instructions.

1. Layer and baste the quilt. Quilt by hand or machine.

2. Finish the quilt.

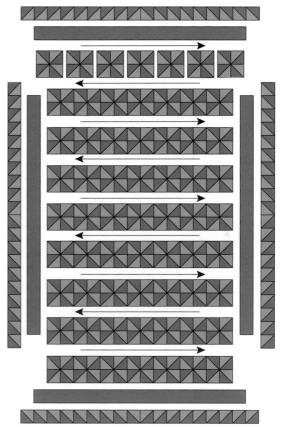

Quilt assembly

triangles all around

Triangles All Around, 70½″ × 70½″, made by Cheryl Malkowski

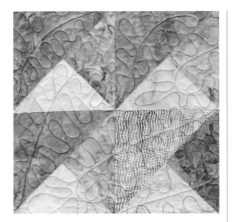

Have fun varying the colors within a block as I did using two different light greens in the E and F blocks.

Fabric Requirements

Fabric Requirements: Yardage is based on 42″-wide fabric unless noted.	
Fabric	**Amount**
Gold	⅝ yd
Fuchsia	⅝ yd
Dark green	⅞ yd
Bright blue	⅝ yd
Purple	⅝ yd
Green	1 yd
Blue	⅝ yd
Yellow	⅝ yd
Light green	⅞ yd
Pale yellow	½ yd
Pale green	½ yd
Aqua	⅝ yd
Fuchsia (for inner border)	⅜ yd
Gold (for middle border)	¼ yd
Blue (for outer border)	1 yd
Purple (for binding)	⅝ yd
Batting	75″ × 75″
108″-wide backing	2⅛ yds

Cutting for Blocks

Cutting Blocks: Strips are cut across width of fabric, selvage to selvage.	
Fabric	**70½″ × 70½″ Quilt**
Gold	• From 2 strips 7½″ wide, cut 6 squares 7½″ × 7½″
Fuchsia	• From 2 strips 7½″ wide, cut 6 squares 7½″ × 7½″
Dark green	• From 3 strips 7″ wide, cut 12 squares 7″ × 7″
Bright blue	• From 2 strips 7½″ wide, cut 10 squares 7½″ × 7½″
Purple	• From 2 strips 7½″ wide, cut 10 squares 7½″ × 7½″
Green	• From 4 strips 7″ wide, cut 18 squares 7″ × 7″
Blue	• From 2 strips 7½″ wide, cut 8 squares 7½″ × 7½″
Yellow	• From 2 strips 7½″ wide, cut 8 squares 7½″ × 7½″
Light green	• From 3 strips 7″ wide, cut 14 squares 7″ × 7″
Pale yellow	• From 1 strip 7½″ wide, cut 4 squares 7½″ × 7½″
Pale green	• From 1 strip 7½″ wide, cut 4 squares 7½″ × 7½″
Aqua	• From 2 strips 7″ wide, cut 6 squares 7″ × 7″

Block Construction

	Block Construction: Sketch numbered blocks and glue small pieces of fabric to them to remind you of your color placement. Follow the directions for making Y blocks on pages 99–101.
	70½″ × 70½″ Quilt
Finished block size	6″ × 6″
Position 1 & 2 square size	7½″ × 7½″
Position 3 square size	7″ × 7″

Block	Diagram	Instructions
Block A		Make 12 from: 3 Position 1 & 2 6 Position 3
Block B		Make 12 from: 3 Position 1 & 2 6 Position 3
Block C		Make 18 from: 5 Position 1 & 2 9 Position 3 (yields 2 extra 1 & 2 units)
Block D		Make 18 from: 5 Position 1 & 2 9 Position 3 (yields 2 extra 1 & 2 units)
Block E		Make 14 from: 4 Position 1 & 2 7 Position 3 (yields 2 extra 1 & 2 units)
Block F		Make 14 from: 4 Position 1 & 2 7 Position 3 (yields 2 extra 1 & 2 units)
Block G		Make 6 from: 2 Position 1 & 2 3 Position 3 (yields 2 extra 1 & 2 units)
Block H		Make 6 from: 2 Position 1 & 2 3 Position 3 (yields 2 extra 1 & 2 units)

Quilt Assembly

Row 1	G	G	E	E	C	D	F	F	H	H
Row 2	G	E	E	C	C	D	D	F	F	H
Row 3	E	E	C	C	A	B	D	D	F	F
Row 4	E	C	C	A	A	B	B	D	D	F
Row 5	C	C	A	A	A	B	B	B	D	D
Row 6	D	D	B	B	B	A	A	A	C	C
Row 7	F	D	D	B	B	A	A	C	C	E
Row 8	F	F	D	D	B	A	C	C	E	E
Row 9	H	F	F	D	D	C	C	E	E	G
Row 10	H	H	F	F	D	C	E	E	G	G

Borders and Binding: Strips are cut across width of fabric, selvage to selvage.	
Fabric	**70½″ × 70½″ Quilt**
Fuchsia	• Join 7 strips 1½″ wide; cut: 2 pieces 60½″ long 2 pieces 62½″ long
Gold	• Join 7 strips ¾″ wide; cut: 2 pieces 62½″ long 2 pieces 63″ long
Blue	• Join 7 strips 4½″ wide; cut: 2 pieces 63″ long 2 pieces 71″ long
Binding	• Cut 8 strips 2″ wide

Making the Blocks

Note that the Position 1 and Position 2 fabrics reverse while the Position 3 fabric remains the same in block sets A & B, C & D, E & F, and G & H. Place each block type in its own zippered bag to keep everything in order while you work.

Putting the Quilt Top Together

1. Assemble the rows using the Quilt Assembly chart, diagram, and project photo as guides. Alternate the pressing direction for each row.

2. Stitch the rows together and press the seams to one side to complete the quilt center.

Borders

1. Use the Borders and Binding chart to prepare the 1½″-wide fuchsia inner border strips. Cut the strips according to the chart or match the measurements of your quilt center.

2. Stitch the 2 short inner border pieces to the top and bottom of the quilt and the 2 long pieces to the sides of the quilt. Press toward the outside.

3. Repeat Steps 1 and 2 for the ¾″-wide gold border strips and the 4½″-wide blue border strips.

Quilting and Finishing

Refer to pages 106–108 for quilting and finishing instructions.

1. Layer and baste the quilt. Quilt by hand or machine.

2. Finish the quilt.

Star of Hope

Star of Hope, 34½˝ × 40½˝ , made by Alex Anderson and machine quilted by Paula Reid

This sea shell fabric really struck me when I saw it in the quilt shop. It had the wonderful melon color and I liked how the fabric designer mixed the browns and pinks with the melon. Looking for interesting prints, I picked fabrics that related to all the different colors in the shell fabric. This method of fabric selection is called using a focus fabric. You are letting the fabric designer inspire the color selection for you.

Fabric Requirements

Yardage is based on 42˝-wide fabric.

Dark stars and border: ⅛ yard each of 10 different browns

Melon star tips and border: ⅛ yard each of 6 melon fabrics

Background: 1 yard off-white

Alternate squares and border: ½ yard focus fabric

Backing: 1¼ yards

Binding: ¼ yard total of assorted browns

Batting: 38˝ × 44˝

Cutting

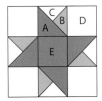

Star of Hope block

Brown stars

Cut 1 strip 2⅞˝ × 42˝ from each of the 10 brown fabrics.

Cut 6 squares 2⅞˝ × 2⅞˝ from each strip (60 total), then cut in half diagonally (half-square triangles) (A).

Cut 3 squares 2⅞˝ × 2⅞˝ from 4 strips and 2 squares 2⅞˝ × 2⅞˝ from 6 strips (need only 21 total), then cut in half diagonally (half-square triangles). Set these aside to be used in the border.

Trim the remaining strips to 2½˝ wide and cut 3 squares 2½˝ × 2½˝ (E) from each strip (30 total).

Melon star tips

Cut 1 strip 3¼˝ × 42˝ from each of the 6 melon fabrics.

Cut 5 squares 3¼˝ × 3¼˝ from each strip (30 total), then cut in half diagonally twice (quarter-square triangles) (B). Set aside the leftover fabric for the border.

Background

Cut 3 strips 3¼˝ × 42˝ of off-white.

Cut 12 squares 3¼˝ from each strip (need only 30 total), then cut in half diagonally twice (quarter-square triangles) (C).

Cut 4 strips 2⅞˝ × 42˝ of off-white.

Cut 12 squares 2⅞˝ from each strip (need only 40 total), then cut in half diagonally (half-square triangles) (F).

Cut 3 strips 2½˝ × 42˝.

Cut 14 squares (D) 2½˝ from each strip (need only 40 total).

Focus fabric

Cut 2 strips 3⅜˝ × 42˝ from focus fabric.

Cut 10 squares (G) 3⅜˝ from each strip (20 total). Set aside leftover fabric for the border.

Making the Blocks

Use a ¼˝ seam allowance. Press following the arrows. Press all seams open where 2 (C) shapes come together. Accurate stitching is necessary in order for the pieced border to fit.

1. Arrange the star points and squares, background triangles and squares, and focus fabric squares. Use the photo as a guide.

2. Sew together the background and melon quarter-square triangle (B/C) units, then join to the 2⅞″ brown triangles (A). Place these units back in the arrangement.

Press following the arrows.

3. Sew the 2½″ half-square background triangles (F) to the 3⅜″ focus fabric squares (G). Place these units back in the arrangement.

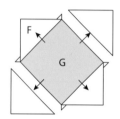

Press following the arrows.

Putting the Quilt Top Together

Sew the pieces in rows as shown and press following the arrows. Note that each individual star isn't formed until the rows are sewn together. Press.

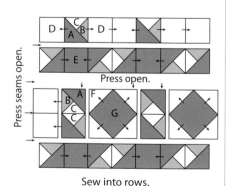

Sew into rows.

Your quilt top should measure 30½″ × 36½″.

BORDER

1. Trim the 6 leftover melon fabric strips to 2⅞″ wide.

2. Cut 3 squares 2⅞″ from 1 strip and 2 squares 2⅞″ from 5 strips (13 total), then cut in half diagonally (half-square triangles).

3. Gather the brown half-square triangles that were set aside to be used for the border.

4. Cut 3 strips 2⅞″ × 42″ of focus fabric.

5. Cut 12 squares 2⅞″ from each strip (need only 34 total), then cut in half diagonally (half-square triangles).

6. Trim 1 of these remaining strips to 2½″ wide and cut 2 squares 2½″.

7. Pair a focus fabric triangle with each brown and melon triangle and stitch to form 64 border squares.

8. Arrange in a pleasing manner around the quilt.

9. Stitch 16 border squares together. Add a 2½″ focus fabric square to one end. Add to the top edge of the quilt top with the square on the left. Repeat for the bottom border, with the square on the right.

Quilting and Finishing

Refer to pages 106–108 for quilting and finishing instructions.

1. Layer and baste the quilt. Quilt by hand or machine.

2. Finish the quilt.

Quilt construction

amish baskets

Amish Baskets, 38½˝ × 38½˝, made by Alex Anderson

A series of borders in varying sizes and corner squares create visual interest. The Cake Stand blocks are simpler "cousins" of the center block, and help to unify the overall design. A narrow, folded piping adds pizzazz to the straightforward mitered binding.

Materials

Fabric amounts are based on a 42"-wide fabric.

Yellow check: ¼ yard for Basket block

Assorted rosy-red prints: ⅓ yard total for Basket and Cake Stand blocks

Assorted yellow prints: ⅛ yard total for Basket block

Yellow and rosy-red small print: ⅓ yard for Basket block and corner squares

Yellow and rosy-red large-scale print: 1¼ yards for setting triangles and outer border

Red check: ⅓ yard for inner border and folded piping

Rosy-red tone-on-tone print: 1 yard for middle border, Cake Stand blocks, and binding*

Yellow print: ¼ yard for Cake Stand blocks

Batting: 42" × 42"

Backing: 1¼ yards

* You can use leftover scraps for Basket block.

Cutting

Yellow check

Cut 1 square 4⅞" × 4⅞", then cut in half diagonally. You'll need 1 triangle for the Basket block (E).

Cut 4 squares 2⅞" × 2⅞", then cut in half diagonally. You'll need 8 triangles for the Basket block (A).

Cut 2 strips 2½" × 8½" for the Basket block (D).

Cut 1 square 2½" × 2½" for the Basket block (B).

Assorted rosy-red prints

Cut a total of 10 squares 2⅞" × 2⅞", then cut in half diagonally. You'll need 20 triangles for the Basket block (A).

Cut a total of 2 squares 3⅞" × 3⅞", then cut in half diagonally. You'll need 4 triangles for the Cake Stand blocks (I).

Assorted yellow prints

Cut 3 squares 2⅞" × 2⅞", then cut in half diagonally. You'll need 6 triangles for the Basket block (A).

Yellow and rosy-red small print

Cut 1 square 8⅞" × 8⅞", then cut in half diagonally. You'll need 1 triangle for the Basket block (C).

Cut 4 squares 2" × 2" for the corner squares.

Cut 4 squares 3½" × 3½" for the corner squares.

Yellow and rosy-red large-scale print

Cut 2 squares 9⅜" × 9⅜", then cut in half diagonally. You'll need 4 for the setting triangles (F).

Cut 4 strips 6½" × the fabric width for the outer border.

Red check

Cut 2 strips 2" × the fabric width for the inner border. Cut each strip in half.

Cut 4 strips 1" × the fabric width for the piping.

Rosy-red tone-on-tone print

Cut 2 strips 3½" × the fabric width for the middle border. Cut each strip in half.

Cut 4 strips 2⅛" × the fabric width for the binding.

Cut 2 squares 3⅞″ × 3⅞″, then cut in half diagonally. You'll need 4 triangles for the Cake Stand blocks (I).

Cut 8 squares 2⅜″ × 2⅜″, then cut in half diagonally. You'll need 16 triangles for the Cake Stand blocks (G).

Cut 1 strip 2″ × the fabric width, then cut into 8 strips 2″ × 3½″ (J) and 4 squares 2″ × 2″ (H) for the Cake Stand blocks.

Yellow print

Cut 2 squares 3⅞″ × 3⅞″, then cut in half diagonally. You'll need 4 triangles for the Cake Stand blocks (I).

Cut 12 squares 2⅜″ × 2⅜″, then cut in half diagonally. You'll need 24 triangles for the Cake Stand blocks (G).

Making the Blocks

Use ¼″ seam allowances. Press in the direction of the arrows.

BASKET BLOCK

1. Stitch yellow check and assorted rosy-red print A triangles in pairs; press. Make 8. Stitch in groups of 4 as shown; press. Make 1 of each.

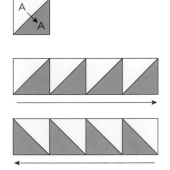

Stitch in pairs, then stitch in groups of 4.

2. Stitch assorted yellow print and rosy-red print A triangles in pairs; press. Make 6. Arrange with assorted rosy-red print A triangles in rows as shown. Stitch the units and triangles into rows; press. Stitch the rows together; press.

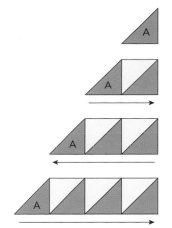

Stitch the units and triangles into rows, then stitch the rows together.

3. Stitch yellow check strips to rosy-red print A triangles as shown; press. Make 1 of each.

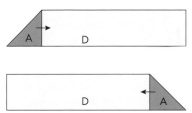

Stitch strips and triangles.

4. Arrange the units from Steps 1–3, the C triangle, the 2½″ yellow check B square, and the E triangle as shown. Sew the block together; press.

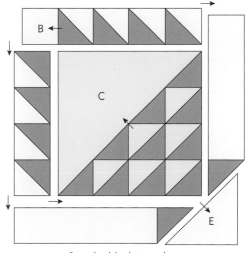

Sew the block together.

5. Stitch a yellow and rosy-red print F triangle to each side of the Basket block; press. The block should now measure approximately 17½˝ × 17½˝.

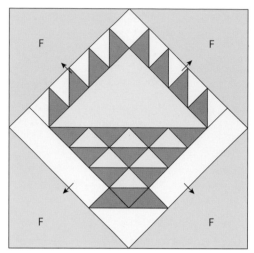

Stitch triangles to Basket block.

CAKE STAND BLOCKS

1. Stitch yellow print and rosy-red tone-on-tone print G triangles in pairs; press. Make 16. Stitch pairs together as shown below; press. Make 4 of each direction.

2. Stitch yellow print and assorted rosy-red print I triangles in pairs; press. Make 4.

3. Stitch rosy-red tone-on-tone print J strips to yellow print G triangles as shown; press. Make 4 of each direction.

4. Arrange the units from Steps 1–3, the 2˝ rosy-red tone-on-tone H square, and the I/I unit as shown. Sew the block together; press. Make 4. The block should measure 6½˝ × 6½˝.

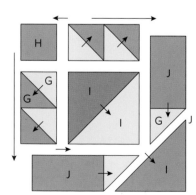

Sew the block together.

Putting the Quilt Top Together

1. Lay out the Basket block, the 2˝ yellow and rosy-red print corner squares, and the red check inner borders as shown in the quilt construction diagram. Stitch the inner border to the quilt. Press.

2. Repeat Step 1 to stitch the 3½˝ yellow and rosy-red print corner squares and the rosy-red tone-on-tone print middle borders to the quilt; press. Add the yellow and rosy-red large-scale print outer borders, positioning the Cake Stand corner blocks as shown in the quilt construction diagram. Press.

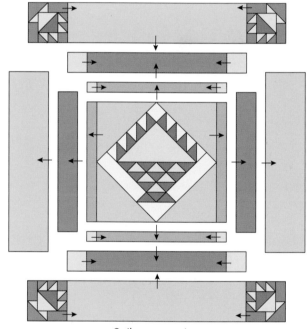

Quilt construction

Quilting and Finishing

Refer to pages 106–108 for quilting and finishing instructions.

1. Layer and baste the quilt. Quilt by hand or machine.

2. Use the 1˝-wide red check strips to make piping as described in Folded Piping (page 98).

betsy's baskets

Betsy's Baskets, 83½˝ × 83½˝, made by Jean Wells and Betsy Mennesson

Pictures of Provence, France, provided the pattern and color ideas for the fabrics in this quilt. The palette is predominantly blues and yellows, with reds and greens popping up in smaller amounts. The plaid inner border was cut on the bias to increase the visual texture.

Materials

Yardage is based on 42″-wide fabric

Basket blocks:

2 yards total assorted white-background prints

¼ yard blue plaid

¼ yard olive green plaid

¼ yard each 2 different dark blue prints

⅛ yard each 4 different textured solids in yellow, red, and blue

Setting triangles:

1⅝ yards total assorted yellow small prints

1 yard total assorted blue small prints

1⅝ yards dark blue print (can match basket fabric)

⅝ yard olive green plaid (can match basket fabric)

½ yard for binding

7½ yards backing

88″ × 88″ batting

Cutting

FRUIT BASKET BLOCKS (25)

Follow the directions to cut pieces A through H for 4 blocks. Repeat the cutting sequence 6 times, using a different combination of fabrics each time. Then cut for 1 more block to bring the block total to 25.

From a plaid or a print, cut 2 squares 6⅞″; cut diagonally in half (A). Cut 4 squares 2⅞″; cut diagonally in half (G).

From the white-background fabric, cut 2 squares 6⅞″; cut diagonally in half (B). Cut 2 strips 2½″ × 42″. Cut into 4 squares (E) 2½″ and 8 rectangles (F) 2½″ × 6½″. Cut 2 squares 4⅞″; cut diagonally in half (H).

From a textured solid and the same white-background print, cut 1 strip each 2⅞″ × 42″. Layer the strips right sides together. Cut into 12 layered 2⅞″ squares; cut diagonally in half for 24 layered triangles (C, D). Do not separate the pairs; they are ready for sewing.

SETTING TRIANGLES

From the assorted small prints, cut 6 yellow and 4 blue 15⅜″ squares; cut diagonally in both directions for 24 yellow and 16 blue setting triangles. Cut 6 yellow and 4 blue 8″ squares; cut diagonally in half for 12 yellow and 8 blue corner triangles.

BORDERS

From the olive green plaid, cut a 21″ square. Following the directions on pages 107–108, make a 1¼″-wide continuous bias strip. Cut into 2 strips 1¼″ × 71⅛″ for the side inner borders and 2 strips 1¼″ × 72⅝″ for the top and bottom inner borders. Avoid stretching the bias edge as you measure and cut.

From the dark blue print, cut 9 strips 6″ × 42″. Sew together into 1 long strip. Cut into 2 strips 6″ × 72⅝″ for the side outer borders and 2 strips 6″ × 83⅝″ for the top and bottom outer borders.

Making the Blocks

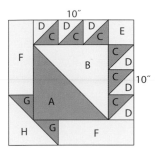

Fruit Basket block

Make 25 assorted.

The Fruit Basket block can be set on point or on its side, as shown here.

1. Stitch the A and B triangles together. Press toward the darker fabric. Trim off the ears.

Make 1.

2. Chain-stitch the C and D triangles together in pairs. Clip apart and press. Trim off the ears. Stitch the CD units together in 2 groups of 3, making 1 set in mirror image. Add an E square to one set as shown. Press.

Make 1.

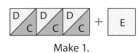

Make 1.

3. Stitch a G to each F, making 2 mirror-image units. Press.

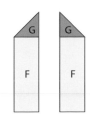

4. Lay out all of the pieced units and triangle H. Stitch the seams in the order shown, pressing after each addition.

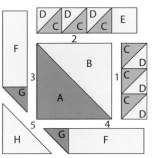

Joining the pieces

Putting the Quilt Top Together

1. Sew pieces A through H together to make 25 Fruit Basket blocks. As you work, swap some of the C pieces between blocks to create multicolored handles.

2. Lay out the blocks on point in 5 columns of 5 blocks each. Place the setting triangles in between, using yellow in columns 1, 3, and 5 and blue in columns 2 and 4, as shown in the quilt photograph (page 33) and quilt diagram. Add the corner triangles to the top and bottom of each column, matching the colors. Adjust the arrangement as needed so similar fabrics are not clustered together.

3. Stitch the yellow and blue setting triangle and corner triangles together along their shared seamlines. Press toward the darker fabric.

4. Stitch the blocks and triangles together in diagonal rows. Press toward the triangles. Join the rows together. Press. Add the 4 remaining corner triangles. Press.

5. Sew the side inner borders to the quilt top, pinning first and being careful not to stretch the bias edge. Press. Sew the top and bottom inner borders. Press. Add the side outer borders. Press. Add the top and bottom outer borders. Press.

Quilting and Finishing

Refer to pages 106–108 for quilting and finishing instructions.

1. Layer and baste the quilt. Quilt by hand or machine.

2. Finish the quilt.

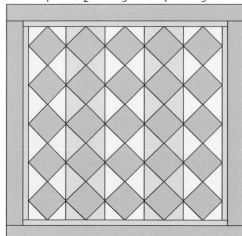

Quilt diagram

sunrise

Sunrise, 25″ × 25″, made by Carol Doak and machine quilted by Kathryn Blais

Cutting for Setting Pieces, Border, and Binding

Cut across the width of the fabric from selvage to selvage.

Fabric	Number to Cut	Size to Cut	Location
Dark green	2	4½″ × 25½″	Top and bottom borders
	2	4½″ × 17½″	Side borders
	3	2¼″ × 40″	Binding
Green/pink print	2	9⅜″ × 9⅜″	Setting triangles

Materials

Yardage is based on 42″-wide fabric.

Dark green: ⅞ yard for border and binding

Green/pink print: ⅜ yard for setting triangles

Maroon: ¼ yard for block

Light green: ⅛ yard for block

Medium green: ⅛ yard for block

Peach: ¼ yard for block

Dark pink: ¼ yard for block

Light pink: ¼ yard for block

Yellow: ⅛ yard for block

Gold: ⅛ yard for block

Backing fabric: ⅞ yard

Batting: 29″ × 29″

Cutting for Block

Fabric	Number to Cut	Size to Cut	Location Number	Sections
Maroon	8	3″ × 3¾″	4	A, B
	8	2¼″ × 3½″	1	A, B
Light green	4	1½″ × 5″	2	A
Medium green	4	1½″ × 5″	2	B
Peach	8	2″ × 5½″	3	A, B
Dark pink	4	2½″ × 8″	5	A
Light pink	4	2½″ × 8″	5	B
Yellow	4	2″ × 4″	6	A
Gold	4	2″ × 4″	6	B

Getting Started

1. Cut and label the fabric pieces as to their location, location numbers, and sections.

2. Make 4 each of the Sections A and B paper foundations (page 39).

Making the Block

(See pages 68–69 for paper-piecing guidance.)

1. Make the 4 A sections and 4 B sections as shown. Join the A and B sections.

Section A

Section B

Make 4.

2. Make the block as shown.

Make 2.

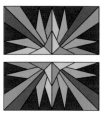

Make 1.

Putting the Quilt Top Together

1. Assemble the quilt top as shown.

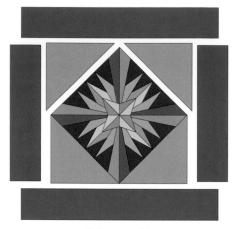

Quilt assembly

2. Remove the paper.

Quilting and Finishing

Refer to pages 106–108 for quilting and finishing instructions.

1. Layer and baste the quilt. Quilt by hand or machine.

2. Finish the quilt.

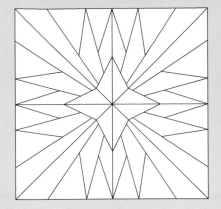

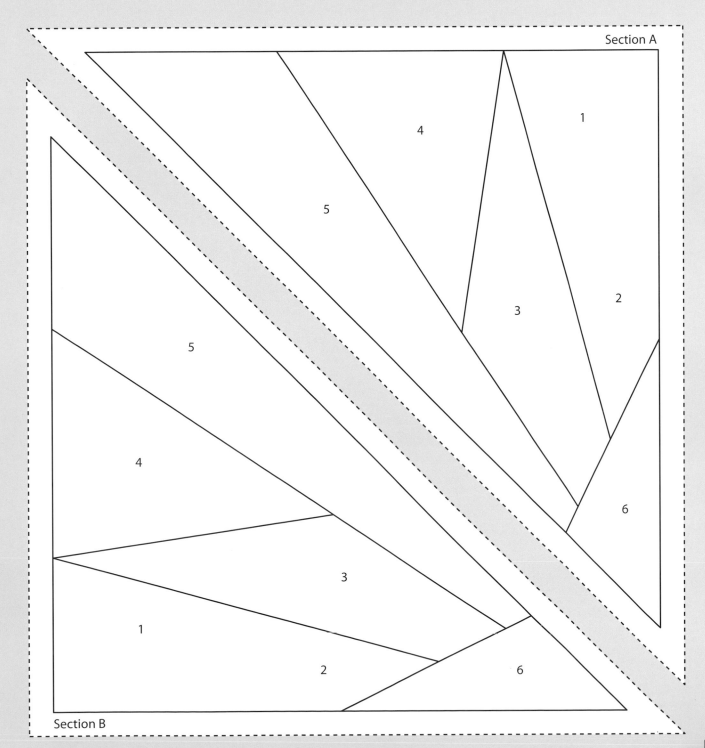

Section A

1

4

5

2

3

6

5

4

3

1

2

6

Section B

sun ray

Sun Ray, 58″ × 62″, made by Alex Anderson and machine quilted by Susanne M. Rasmussen

Stripes and polka dots are the best! I love putting them into my quilts. When I saw this group of fabrics I knew it had my name written all over it. I usually shy away from working with an entire collection because the quilts made entirely from these fabrics can end up looking prepackaged. However, you can solve this dilemma by introducing other fabrics into the set. In this case, I chose to add solids and a few pieces of black-and-white fabric. Even on the gloomiest day this quilt puts a smile on my face!

Materials

The following instructions give the total yardage needed to complete your quilt.

Stars: 2 yards

Background: 2¾ yards

Inner Border: ¼ yard

Outer Border: 1½ yards

Backing: 4 yards

Cutting

6″ SUN RAY

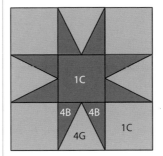

The following numbers are for one 6″ Sun Ray star. You will need 56 in all.

Star Body

Cut one 2½″ square.

Cut a strip 1¾″ by at least 13¼″. Fold and press end to end, like sides together. Cut 4 rectangles 1¾″ × 3¼″. Then cut on the diagonal as shown.

Background

Cut 4 squares 2⅞″, then cut as shown under Background on page 42.

Cut 4 squares 2½″.

Follow the diagram below for piecing sequence. The ^ indicates which edge or point to line up (see All-Star Lineup, page 103). The arrows indicate which way to press.

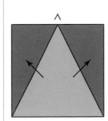

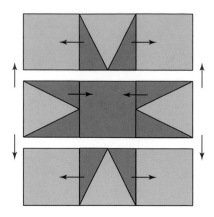

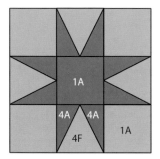

3″ SUN RAY

The following numbers are for one 3″ Sun Ray star. You will need 16 in all.

Star Body

Cut 1 square 1½″.

Cut a strip 1¼″ by at least 9½″. Fold and press end to end, like sides together. Cut 4 rectangles 1¼″ × 2¼″. Then cut on the diagonal as shown.

Background

Cut 4 squares 1⅞″, then cut as shown.

Cut 4 squares (1A) 1½″.

Making the Blocks

Follow the diagram below for piecing sequence. The ∧ indicates which edge or point to line up. The arrows indicate which way to press.

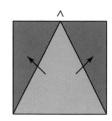

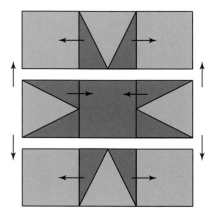

Inner Border

The inner border is 2 different widths in order to accommodate the outer border, which is made up of 2″ blocks.

Cut 2 strips 1″ × 48½″.

Cut 2 strips 1½″ × 46½″.

Outer Border

Cut 324 squares 2½″.

Using the photo on page 40 as your guide, arrange and sew the squares into 3 strips of 25 squares each for the side borders. Press the seams in opposite directions and sew the strips together. Repeat for the top and bottom borders making strips of 29 squares each.

Putting the Quilt Top Together

1. Arrange your blocks as shown.

2. Join your blocks in a straight set, row by row.

3. Sew on the inner borders, making sure the narrow strips are on the sides and the wide strips are on the top and bottom.

4. Sew on the outer checked side borders. Then sew on the outer top and bottom borders.

Quilting and Finishing

Refer to pages 106–108 for quilting and finishing instructions.

1. Layer and baste the quilt. Quilt by hand or machine.

2. Finish the quilt.

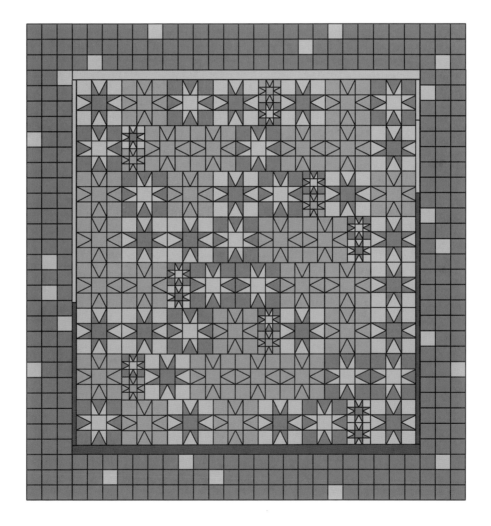

antigua

Antigua, 40″ × 49″, made by Doreen Speckmann

I love this Mutt-and-Jeff Star block and have used it in quite a few quilts. What I had never done was to put three different scales of blocks in the same quilt. It's relatively easy to mix 12˝ and 6˝ blocks. The adventure begins when you add 9˝ blocks. Nothing lines up directly, so we have to employ a "short seam" approach to assembling the whole quilt. I love the random look and new dimension the change of scale gives to each piece. The colors are simple. The stars are made from peachy reds, including a plaid with a little turquoise strip. The background and border are different turquoise blues. What makes this quilt special is the Dutch Java bubble-and-wave fabric that I bought in Antigua. At the time I was aggravated that I had to buy a three-yard sarong piece; now I wish they had made me buy six yards because my supply is running low.

Star Blocks

UNITS

TEMPLATES

Materials

Yardage is based on 42˝-wide fabric.

Assorted blue prints: 1½ yards total

Assorted Peachy Red Prints: 1 yard total

First Border: ⅓ yard

Second Border and Binding: 1⅝ yards

Cutting

For cutting guidance see page 102.

There are three 12″ blocks, three 9″ blocks and six 6″ blocks. Note that one corner in each of the 9″ blocks has been altered to accommodate the weird setting. All the others remain whole.

Fabric	Size/Template	Total
Background (Blues)		
	4½″ × 4½″ (shared)	10
	K4	12
	3½″ × 3½″	8
	K3	12
	2½″ × 2½″	24
	K2	24
Filler strips (Blues)		
Four 2½″ × 6½″ strips		
One 4½″ × 7½″ strip		
Two 1½″ × 9½″ strips		
One 1½″ × 10½″ strip		
One 3½″ × 8½″ strip		
Three 1½″ × 3½″ strips		
Four 1½″ × 2½″ strips		
One 1½″ × 6½″ strip		
One 2½″ × 3½″ strip		
Star Points (Peachy Reds)		
	G4	12
	2⅞″ × 2⅞″; cut in half diagonally	12
	G3	12
	2⅜″ × 2⅜″; cut in half diagonally	12
	G2	24
	1⅞″ × 1⅞″; cut in half diagonally	24
Center Diamond (Peachy Reds)		
	H4	3
	H3	3
	H2	6
Triangles around Diamonds (Peachy Reds)	2⅞″ × 2⅞″; cut in half diagonally	12
	2⅜″ × 2⅜″; cut in half diagonally	12
	1⅞″ × 1⅞″; cut in half diagonally	24
First Border	1½″ × width of fabric	5
Second Border	5½″ × width of fabric	6

Making the Blocks

Piece together the units for all the blocks. Then make all the 6″ blocks. Wait to construct the 9″ and 12″ blocks.

Putting the Quilt Top Together

Here's where it starts to get tricky. (Nothing really lines up into tidy rows, so proceed slowly.) To make this go together you need to sew "short seams" to avoid having set-in pieces.

SHORT SEAM TECHNIQUE

Here's the principle that you may have used before in a traditional block, called Bright Hopes.

1. Sew a square to the first piece, but begin stitching 1″ short of the end.

2. Sew the next 2 strips on as if you were making a Log Cabin block.

3. Flip the loose corner of the first strip away from the edge and sew on the fourth strip.

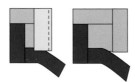

4. Now you can come back to where you originally started the first strip and finish sewing it to the rest of the block. This is harder to explain in words than it is to actually do. But, it's nifty to have in your bag of sewing tricks.

Our goal is never to have to sew into a corner. The method I just described enables us to avoid that. Now for my best advice: Lay the quilt out on a flat vertical surface with all the fill-in pieces in place. Plan only three sewing moves at a time. The worst thing you can do is to get too far ahead of yourself. Look for the seams you can sew from end to end and where you will need to stop short.

Add the first border 1½″ (finished) and the second border 4½″ (finished) to complete the quilt.

Refer to pages 104–105 for mitered borders.

QUILTING AND FINISHING

Refer to pages 106–108 for quilting and finishing instructions.

1. Layer and baste the quilt. Quilt by hand or machine.

2. Finish the quilt.

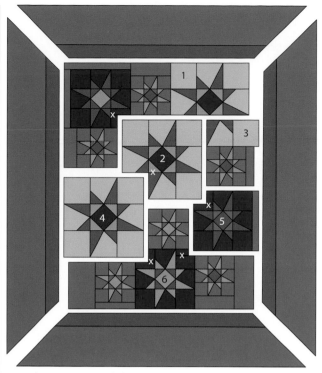

Complete sections and then sew together in numerical order. X marks short seam.

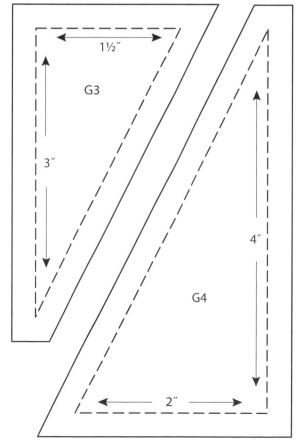

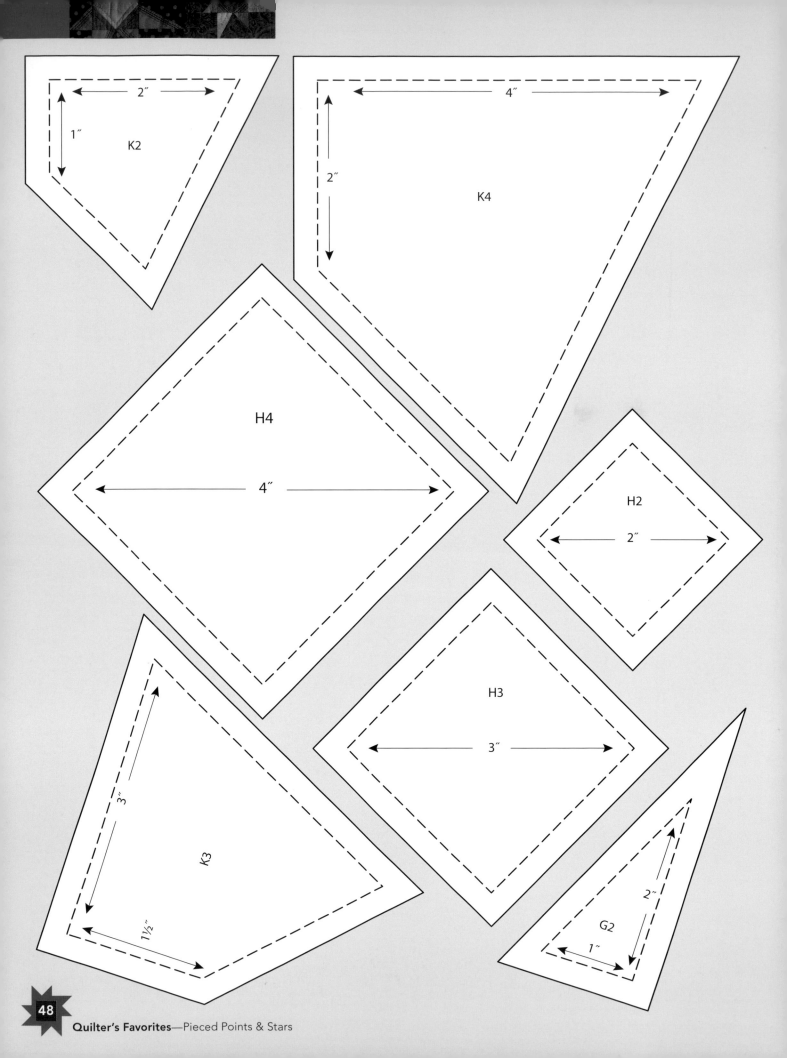

K2

2″

1″

K4

4″

2″

H4

4″

H2

2″

H3

3″

K3

3″

1½″

G2

2″

1″

grand cayman

Grand Cayman, 36″ × 36″, made by Doreen Speckmann

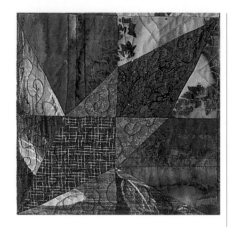

Concentric Lilies

UNITS

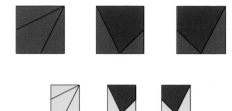

The mini Lily blocks look really great toward the border. The fish seem to be swimming away from the center, and the background fabric reminds me of bubbles in the water.

TEMPLATES

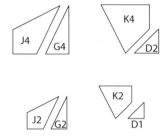

Materials

Yardage is based on 42˝-wide fabric.

I used two background fabrics: the center circle matches the border fabric. A strip of the second background surrounds the pieced part of the quilt to float the lilies at the border's edge. Choose any floral colors that show up on the background fabric. I used colors that remind me of the Caribbean: pinks, oranges, and yellows.

Blue for Center Background, Outer Border, and Binding: 1¼ yards

Blue for Outer Background and Inner Border: ¾ yard

Orange Prints: ½ yard total

Pink Prints: ½ yard total

Yellow Prints: ⅜ yard total

Cutting

For cutting guidance see page 102.

Fabric	Size/Template	Total
Background (center)	K4 (left and right)	8
	G4 (left and right)	8
Background (outer)	K4 (left and right)	8
	K2 (left and right)	16
	G2 (left and right)	16
Orange	J4	4
	2⅞″ × 2⅞″; then cut in half diagonally (D2)	8
	G4 (left and right)	16
Pink	J4	8
	2⅞″ × 2⅞″; then cut in half diagonally (D2)	8
	G4 (left and right)	16
Yellow	J2	16
	1⅞″ × 1⅞″; then cut in half diagonally (D1)	16
	G2 (left and right)	32
Inner Border	1½″ × width of fabric	4
Outer Border	5½″ × width of fabric	4

Putting the Quilt Top Together

Assemble the units. The center of the quilt should measure 24″ square. Add at least an inch of the outside background to all 4 sides. Add borders, 1″ (finished) and 5″ (finished), mitering the corners, to complete the quilt. *Refer to pages 104–105 for mitered borders.*

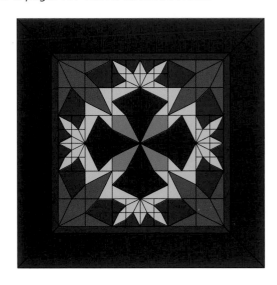

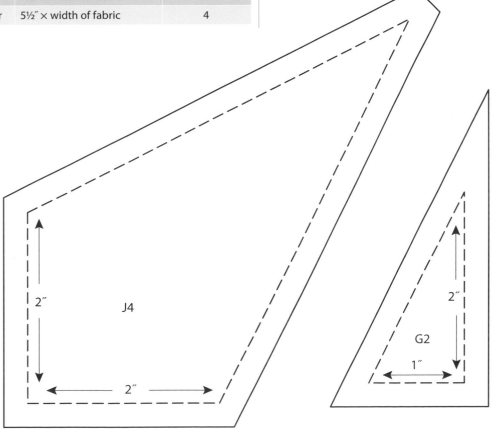

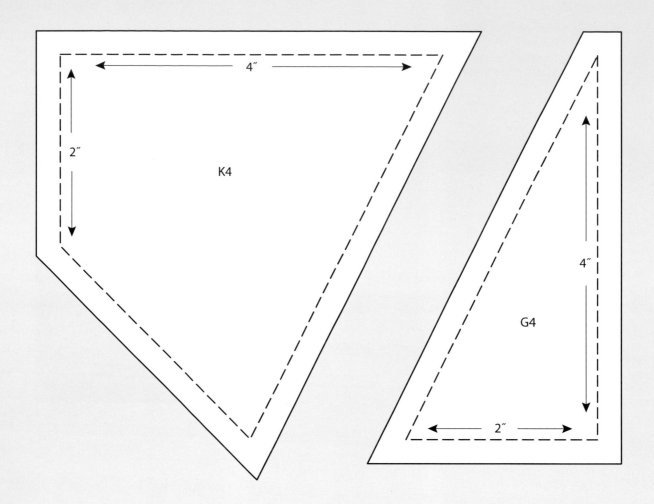

K4

4″

2″

G4

4″

2″

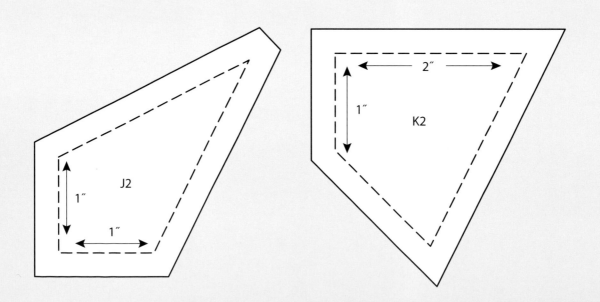

J2

1″

1″

K2

2″

1″

playa del carmen

Playa del Carmen, 28″ × 28″, made by Doreen Speckman and machine quilted by Gayle Wallace

My goal here was to put both Little Fish and Long Fish blocks into one quilt. I'm not even sure you can tell they are fish, but I liked the design and the opportunity to use really wild fabric. Obviously I was not trying for subtle and tasteful when choosing colors for this small piece, so I assembled a group of seven fabrics based on yellow and orange or orange and red. The Long Fish fabric, with its four ribbons of turquoise, is ideal in this design. I found this fabric in Australia (a Jimmy Pike design). The two turquoise blues cool things down so you can stand to look at the quilt. I think the overall design would be just as effective using softer colors.

MAKING THE BLOCKS

TEMPLATES

A4 F4 D2 L4 G4

Q4 I-4 H4

Materials

Yardage is based on 42"-wide fabric.

Turquoise 1 for Center Background and Binding: ⅞ yard

Turquoise 2 for Outer Border: ½ yard

Yellow/Orange Check: ⅛ yard

Yellow/Orange Spotted Print: ½ yard

Orange/Yellow Swirly Print: ½ yard

Paisley Print: ⅓ yard

Shaded Orange Print: ¼ yard

Purple/Orange Check: ¼ yard

Cutting

For cutting guidance see page 102.

Fabric	Size/Templates	Total
Turquoise 1 (Center Background)	4½″ × 4½″	4
	L4	8
	G4 (left and right)	8
Turquoise 2 (Outer Border)	G4 (left and right)	32
	2⅞″ × 2⅞″; cut in half diagonally (D2)	28
Yellow/Orange Check	2⅞″ × 2⅞″; cut in half diagonally (D2)	8
Yellow/Orange Spotted Print	L4	4
	G4 (left and right)	8
	2⅞″ × 2⅞″; cut in half diagonally (D2)	16
Orange/Yellow Swirly Print	Q4	8
	I-4	8
Paisley Print	L4	4
	H4	1
	G4 (left and right)	8
Shaded Orange Print	F4	4
	G4 (left and right)	8
Purple/Orange Check	2⅞″ × 2⅞″; cut in half diagonally (D2)	8
	F4	4

Putting the Quilt Top Together

Assemble all the units. Join them as shown in the illustration, to complete the quilt.

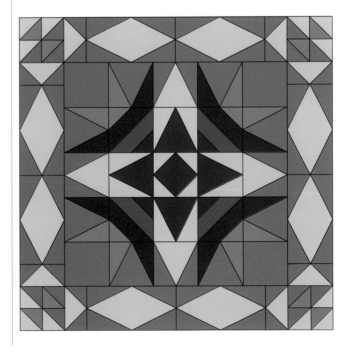

QUILTING AND FINISHING

Refer to pages 106–108 for quilting and finishing instructions.

1. Layer and baste the quilt. Quilt by hand or machine.

2. Finish the quilt.

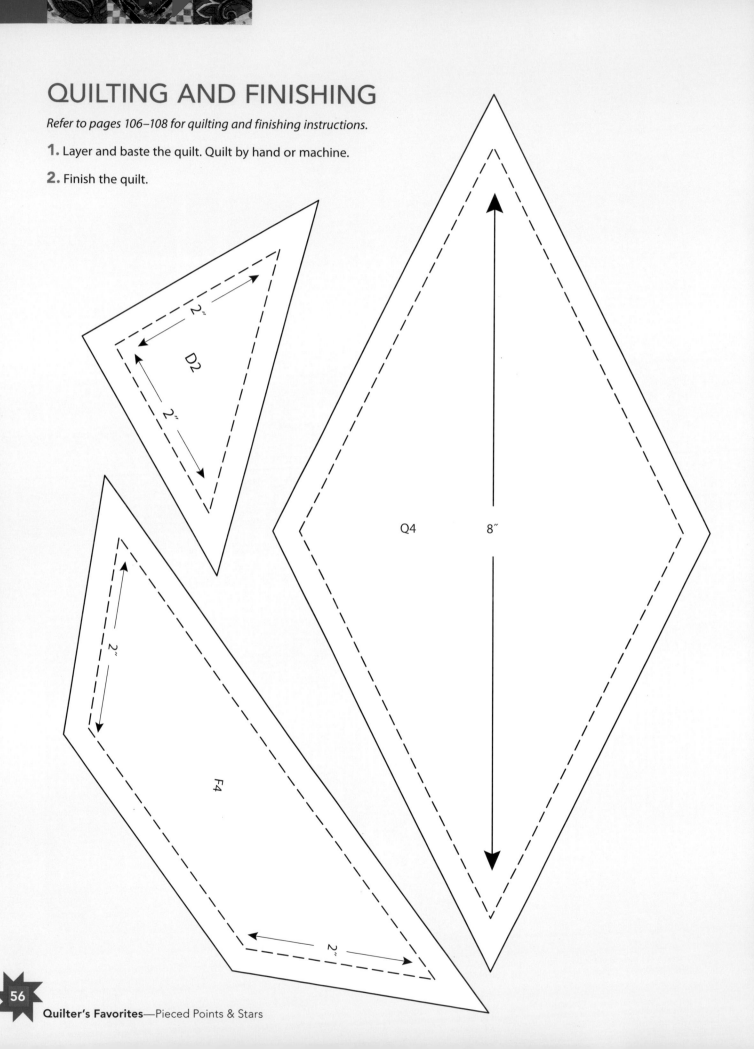

Quilter's Favorites—Pieced Points & Stars

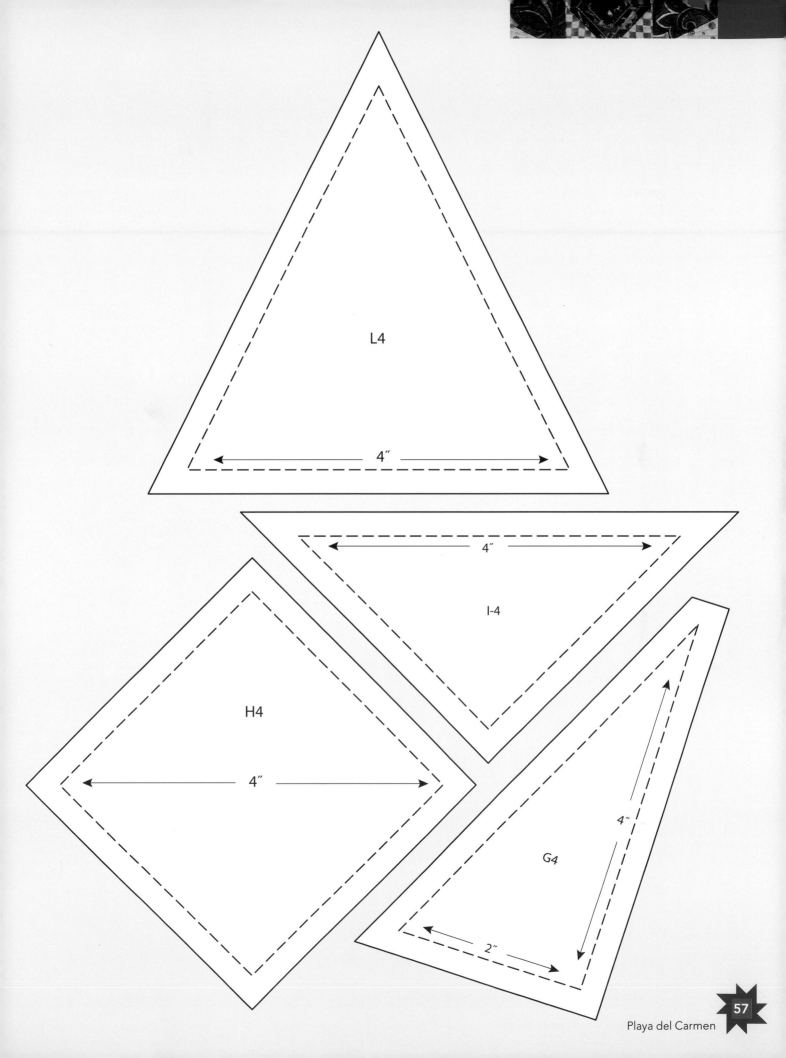

L4

4″

I-4

4″

H4

4″

G4

4″

2″

Curve-azy Stars

Curve-azy Stars, 74˝ × 86˝, made by Peggy J. Barkle

I love the look of this quilt, particularly the floating squares that result when two stars lie next to each other. Another fun element is the pink butterfly unit formed where the tips of two half-square triangles touch. The quilt is visually striking because each star is made of a different fabric. No two stars are alike, just like in the night sky.

Materials

Yardage is based on a 42˝-wide fabric width and strips cut from selvage to selvage on the crosswise grain, unless otherwise noted.

1½ yards total yellow and orange fabrics (For ease, instructions use only 1 yellow/orange for the floating squares.)

1 fat quarter each of 30 different star fabrics

1⅝ yards background fabric

½ yard pink fabric

⅜ yard inner-border fabric*

2¼ yards outer-border fabric* (strips cut on lengthwise grain)

⅞ yard bias-binding fabric for 2½˝-wide double-fold binding

5¼ yards backing fabric (seam to run the length of grain)

80˝ × 92˝ batting

* Border yardage based on butted borders, sides sewn on first.

Cutting

Cut all strips from selvage to selvage.

Yellow Squares

From the yellow fabric, cut 11 strips 4½˝ wide. Subcut the strips into 98 squares 4½˝ × 4½˝.

Star Squares

From each of the 30 star fabrics, cut 1 square 6½˝ × 6½˝ for the star centers.

From each of the 30 star fabrics, cut 4 squares 4½˝ × 4½˝ for the star points.

From the background fabric, cut 3 strips 4½˝ wide. Subcut the strips into 22 squares 4½˝ × 4½˝ for the star points.

From the background fabric, cut 7 strips 3½˝ wide. Subcut the strips into 80 squares 3½˝ × 3½˝ for the star block corners.

Pink Butterfly Corners

From the pink butterfly fabric, cut 3 strips 4½˝ wide. Subcut the strips into 20 squares 4½˝ × 4½˝.

From the background fabric, cut 3 strips 4½˝ wide. Subcut the strips into 20 squares 4½˝ × 4½˝.

Making the Blocks

The trick to this quilt is keeping track of all the elements. Notice in the photo (page 58) for instance, that the interior star points are paired with a different fabric than the perimeter star points. For this quilt, having a large working space or a design board really helps. Lay out your pieces as you go, referring to the assembly diagram (page 61).

CREATING THE BLENDABLE CURVE

Cut solid squares in 2 colors and stack a pair together **right sides up**. Use a sharp rotary cutter to cut your free-form Blendable Curve from corner to opposite corner and move one half of the top block to the corresponding bottom position. This shuffling will give you 2 new half-square triangle blocks that are a combination of your original 2 colors.

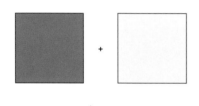

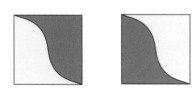

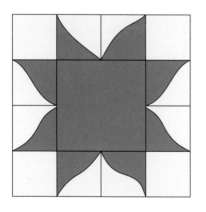

PINK BUTTERFLY CORNERS

Pair the 20 pink squares 4½″ × 4½″ with 20 background-fabric squares, right sides up, in sets of 2. Stack, slice, shuffle, and sew. You will have

40 star corners. Press toward the pink fabric. Square the blocks to 3½″ × 3½″.

Make 40.

CORNER STAR BLOCKS

1. Select 4 matching star-fabric squares, 4½″ × 4½″. Pair 2 of these with 2 yellow/orange squares, right sides up, in sets of 2. Stack, slice, shuffle, and sew. You will have 4 star points. Press toward the star fabric. Square the blocks to 3½″ × 3½″.

2. Pair the other 2 matching star-fabric squares 4½″ × 4½″ with 2 background-fabric squares, right sides up, in sets of 2. Stack, slice, shuffle, and sew. You will have 4 star points. Press toward the star fabric. Square the blocks to 3½″ × 3½″.

3. Repeat Steps 1 and 2 to make 3 more sets of 8 matching star points.

4. Assemble the corner star blocks as illustrated below, using 1 matching star square 6½″ × 6½″ in the center and the star points prepared above. Two of the corner star blocks will have a pink butterfly block in 1 of their corners, and 2 will have all background fabric corners.

Make 2.   Make 2.

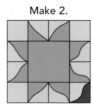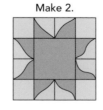

PERIMETER STAR BLOCKS

1. Select 4 matching star-fabric squares, 4½″ × 4½″. Pair 3 of these with 3 yellow/orange squares, right sides up, in sets of 2. Stack, slice, shuffle, and sew. You will have 6 star points. Press toward the star fabric. Square the blocks to 3½″ × 3½″.

2. Pair the 1 remaining star square with 1 background-fabric square, right sides up. Stack, slice, shuffle, and sew. You will have 2 star points. Press toward the star fabric. Square the blocks to 3½″ × 3½″.

3. Repeat Steps 1 and 2 to make 13 more sets of 8 matching star points.

4. Assemble the perimeter star blocks as illustrated below, using 1 matching star square 6½″ × 6½″ in the center and the star points prepared above. Press toward the star fabric. Seven of the perimeter star blocks will have pink butterfly blocks in 2 of the corner positions and 7 will have all background fabric corners.

Make 7.   Make 7.

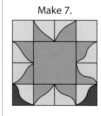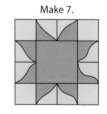

INTERIOR STAR BLOCKS

1. Select 4 matching star fabric squares, 4½″ × 4½″. Pair these with 4 yellow /orange squares, right sides up, in sets of 2. Stack, slice, shuffle, and sew. You will have 8 star points. Press toward the star fabric. Square the blocks to 3½″ × 3½″.

2. Repeat Step 1 to make 11 more sets of 8 matching star points.

3. Assemble the interior star blocks as illustrated below, using 1 matching star square 6½″ × 6½″ in the center and the star points prepared above. Press toward the star fabric. Six of the interior star blocks will have pink butterfly blocks in each corner and 6 will have all background fabric corners.

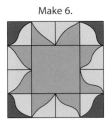
Make 6.

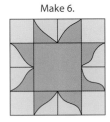
Make 6.

Putting the Quilt Top Together

Use the assembly diagram to assemble the blocks into the quilt top and press well. Keep in mind that the colors of the stars in the diagram may not match yours, depending on the 30 star fabrics you choose. Apply a 1½″ cut-width inner border and a 6½″ cut-width outer border using your favorite border application method.

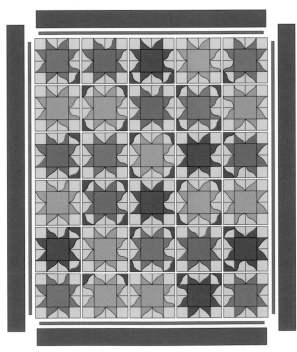
Assembly diagram

Quilting and Finishing

Refer to pages 106–108 for quilting and finishing instructions.

1. Layer and baste the quilt. Quilt by hand or machine.

2. Finish the quilt.

Notes on Quilting

I chose a soft-edged allover pantograph pattern because I felt that a stylized quilting design would not enhance the quilt's finished look. I wanted the thread to have some impact on the quilt, so I chose a lime green thread to show up in the darker stars.

Splash quilting motif, copyright © 2004 by Jodi Beamish of Willow Leaf Studio Designs

hot, hot, hot!

intermediate

Finished block size: 12″

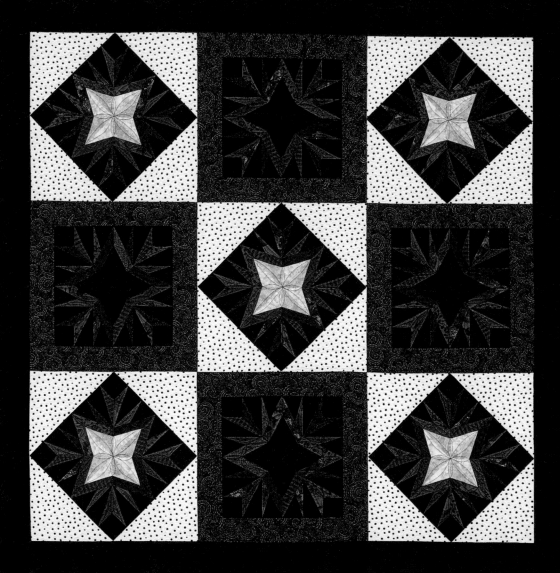

Hot, Hot, Hot!, 63″ × 63″, made by Carol Doak and machine quilted by Kathryn Blais

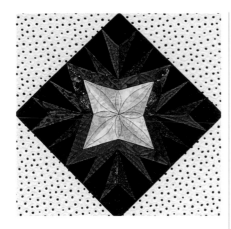

Cutting for Setting Pieces, Borders, and Binding

Cut the outer border pieces and binding lengthwise, parallel to the selvages, and cut the remaining pieces across the width of the fabric from selvage to selvage.

Fabric	Number to Cut	Size to Cut	Location
Black	2	6½″ × 51½″	Side outer borders
	2	6½″ × 63½″	Top and bottom outer borders
	5	2¼″ × 55″	Binding
Red/gold print	8	3″ × 12½″	Block side borders
	8	3″ × 17½″	Block top and bottom borders
Black-and-white dot	10	9⅜″ × 9⅜″ ◻	Setting triangles

Materials

Yardage is based on 42″-wide fabric.

Black: 4 yards for outer border, binding, and blocks

Black-and-white dot: 1⅛ yards for setting triangles

Red/gold print: ¾ yard for block side, top, and bottom borders

8 assorted reds: ¼ yard each for blocks

Gold: ⅜ yard for blocks

Yellow: ⅜ yard for blocks

Backing fabric: 3¾ yards

Batting: 67″ × 67″

Cutting for Blocks

Fabric	Number to Cut	Size to Cut	Location Number	Sections
Black	36	3¼″ × 3¼″ ◻	3	A, B
	32	3″ × 5″	7	A, B
	72	2¾″ × 5″	1	A, B
	72	2¾″ × 3½″	5	A, B
8 assorted reds*	72	1½″ × 5½″	2	A, B
	72	1½″ × 5″	4	A, B
	72	1½″ × 6″	6	A, B
Gold	20	3″ × 5″	7	A
Yellow	20	3″ × 5″	7	B

Cut 9 pieces of each size from each of the 8 assorted red fabrics for a total of 72 pieces.

Getting Started

1. Cut and label the fabric pieces as to their location, location numbers, and sections.

2. Make 36 each of the Sections A and B paper foundations (page 65).

Making the Blocks

(See pages 68–69 for paper piecing guidance.)

1. Make the 16 A sections and 16 B sections as shown. Join the A and B sections.

Section A

Section B

Make 16.

2. Make 4 blocks as shown.

Make 8.

Make 4.

3. Join the side and top and bottom borders to the 4 blocks.

Make 4.

4. Make 20 A sections and 20 B sections as shown. Repeat Steps 1 and 2 to join the A and B sections and make 5 blocks.

Section A

Section B

Make 20.   Make 5.

5. Join the setting triangles to the 5 blocks.

Make 5.

Putting the Quilt Top Together

1. Assemble the quilt top as shown.

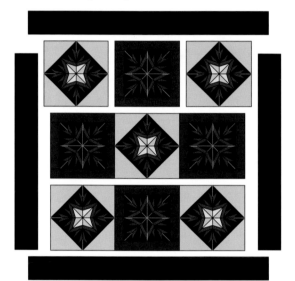

Quilt assembly

2. Remove the paper.

Quilting and Finishing

Refer to pages 106–108 for quilting and finishing instructions.

1. Layer and baste the quilt. Quilt by hand or machine.

2. Finish the quilt.

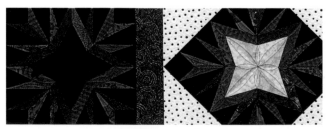

Quilting suggestion

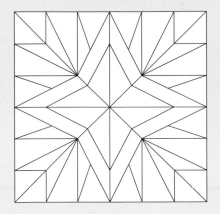

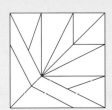

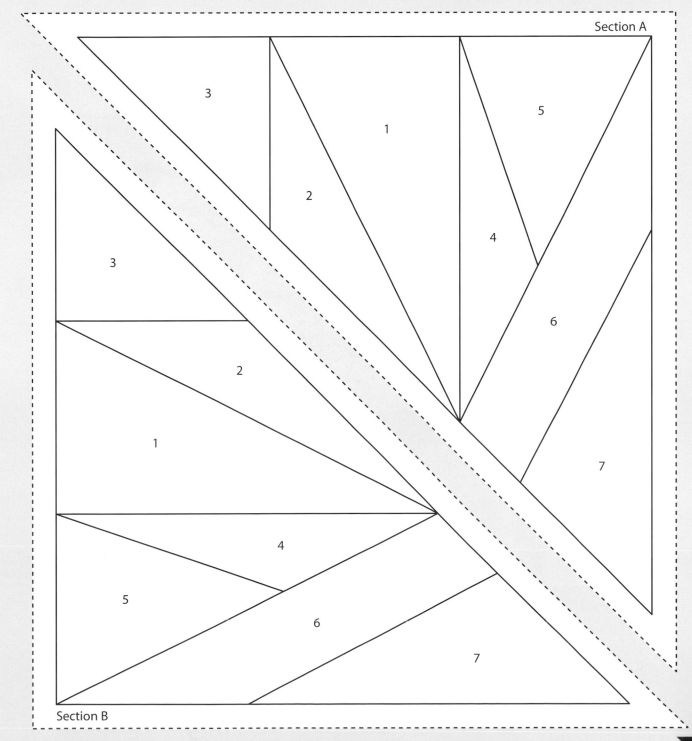

Section A

Section B

floral stars

Floral Stars, 35″ × 35″, made by Carol Doak and machine quilted by Kathryn Blais

This quilt features a block design of those wonderful points in a medallion setting that produces a central star.

Materials

Yardage is based on 42″-wide fabric.

Dark green: ⅞ yard for outer border, binding, and blocks

Floral print: ⅞ yard for inner border

Gold: ⅛ yard

Light purple: ¼ yard

Dark purple: ¼ yard

Light green: ¼ yard

Medium green: ⅜ yard

Beige: ⅞ yard

Backing: 1⅛ yards

Batting: 39″ × 39″

Preparing the Foundations

Make 20 copies of the Floral Stars foundation pattern on page 70. Space them at least ½″ apart. If you use a copy machine to reproduce the block designs, make all your copies on the same copy machine from the original and check for accuracy. Trim the paper foundations ½″ from the outside solid line and ¼″ outside the dashed line.

CUTTING THE FABRIC

Cut across the width of the fabric, selvage to selvage.

CUTTING FOR BORDERS AND BINDING

> **note**
>
> The ◩ in the cutting list indicates that a square should be cut that size, then cut in half diagonally to produce 2 half-square triangles.

Fabric	No. to cut	Size to cut	Location
Dark green	2	3″ × 30½″	Side outer border
	2	3″ × 35½″	Top and bottom outer border
	4	2¼″ × 40″	Binding
Floral print	4	5½″ × 20½″	Inner border

Cut the following pieces and label each group with its location.

Cutting for blocks			
Fabric	No. to cut	Size to cut	Location
Gold	20	1½″ × 1½″	1
Light purple	20	1½″ × 2¼″	5
Dark purple	20	2¼″ × 4″	6
Dark green	10	3″ × 3″ ◩	13
Light green	20	2¼″ × 4″	9
Medium green	20	2¼″ × 5¾″	10
Beige	10	3″ × 3″ ◩	4
	80	2¼″ × 4″	7, 8, 11, 12
	20	2″ × 2″ ◩	2, 3

> **tip**
>
> To speed up the process, assembly-line sew the 20 blocks.

Making the Blocks

1. Place the fabric 1 piece right side up on the blank side of the paper over the #1 area. Make sure the fabric extends at least ¼˝ on all sides. Pin in place. Place a pin away from and parallel to the #1 / #2 seamline.

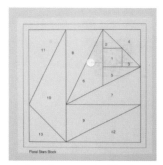

Place fabric right side up on the blank side of the paper.

2. Place a card on the seamline between #1 and #2. Fold the paper back, exposing the excess fabric.

Place the card on the #1/#2 seamline.

Fold the paper back over the card.

3. Place an Add-a-Quarter ruler on the fold and trim the extending fabric ¼˝ from the seamline.

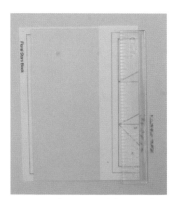

Trimming the excess fabric with an Add-a-Quarter ruler on the fold

4. Place the fabric 2 piece right side up over the area it needs to cover to correctly orient the fabric. Flip it right sides together with fabric 1.

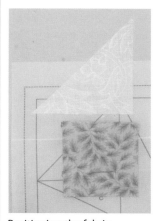
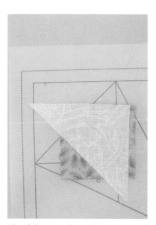

Positioning the fabric right side up

Flip fabric right sides together.

5. Turn the foundation over and sew on the seamline between #1 and #2 (using 18–20 stitches per inch, or 1.5–1.8 metric). Start sewing about ½˝ before the line and extend the stitching line ½˝ beyond the end.

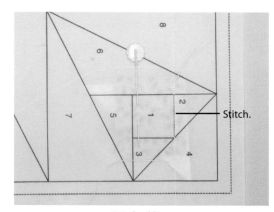

Stitched line

6. Clip the threads and press piece 2 open.

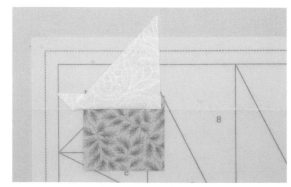

Piece 2 pressed open

7. Continue in the same fashion by placing the card on the next seamline you will sew, the #1/#3 seamline, and folding the paper back. You will need to pull the stitching away from the foundation to do this, and that is OK. Trim the fabric ¼" beyond the fold using the Add-a-Quarter ruler.

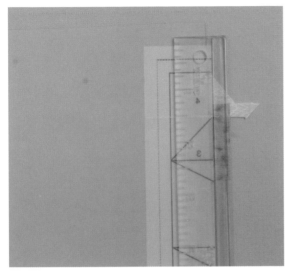

Trimming for piece 3

8. Place the fabric 3 piece right side up over the area it needs to cover to check that it is the right size, flip it right sides together with the just-trimmed edge, turn the foundation over, and sew on the line between #1 and #3. Clip the threads and press piece 3 open.

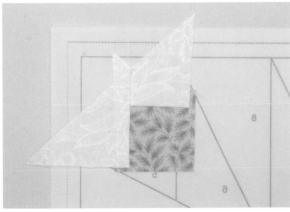

Piece 3 pressed open

9. Continue in the same fashion until all the pieces have been sewn in sequence. Using a rotary cutter, trim the completed foundation on the dashed line (¼" from the outside solid line).

Machine Basting Technique

Now that you have paper pieced perfect blocks, using this machine basting technique will ensure that your blocks will go together perfectly.

1. Place 2 trimmed blocks right sides together. Pin the blocks together, slightly away from the seamline, at the beginning, at the end, and at any matching points on the seamline or at least every 3". Increase the stitch length to 8 stitches per inch and machine baste on the seamline about 1" at each pinned location. Do not cut the threads; just move to the next location.

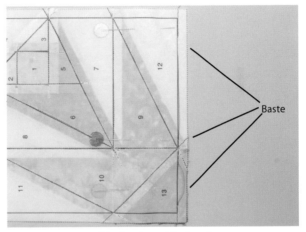

Blocks pinned for basting

2. Open the basted blocks and check for a good match. If you are pleased with the match, sew the seamline (using 18–20 stitches per inch, or 1.5–1.8 metric). If you are not pleased with the match, clip the threads on each side of the location to be adjusted and pull the thread out from the bobbin side. Readjust and baste that location again before sewing with the smaller stitch. From the fabric side, press both seam allowances to the same side of the block.

Open and check for a good match.

Putting the Quilt Top Together

1. Arrange the blocks into rows, stitch, and press the seam allowances in opposing directions. Sew the rows together. Press.

2. Add the corner blocks and inner and outer borders and sew. Press.

3. Starting at the outside edge of the quilt, tug diagonally on each block to pull the paper away from the stitching. Use a pair of tweezers to pull the paper from the underside of each seam allowance.

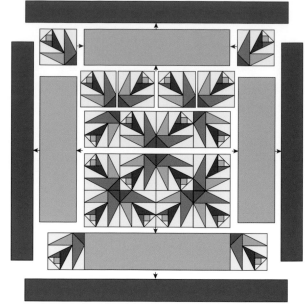

Assembly diagram

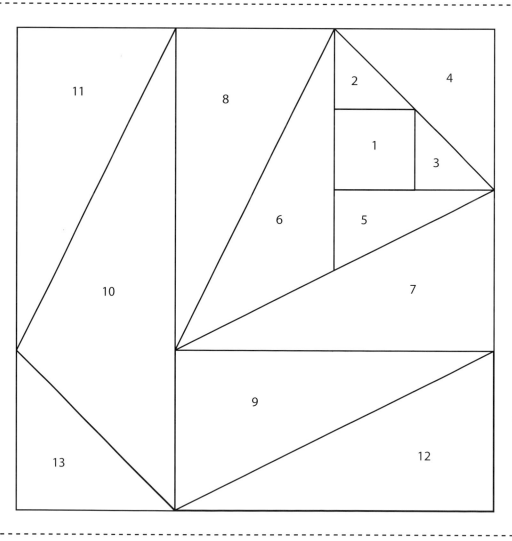

Floral Stars foundation pattern

Quilting and Finishing

Refer to pages 106–108 for quilting and finishing instructions.

1. Layer and baste the quilt. Quilt by hand or machine.

2. Finish the quilt.

primarily stars

intermediate

Finished block size: 12″

Primarily Stars, 82½″ × 82½″, made by Jean Wells

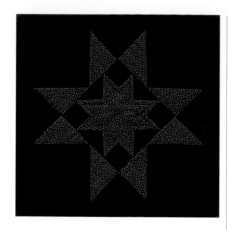

Sawtooth Stars set on point are the key players in this quilt. A 6″ star fits neatly within each 12″ block. To create the smaller floating stars, half-square triangles are added to the ends of the sashing strips. The fabrics for this quilt are heirloom prints. Most are monochromatic.

Materials

Yardage is based on 42″-wide fabric.

7¼ yards black

½ to ⅝ yard each 7 or more small prints in assorted colors

½ yard for binding

7⅜ yards backing

87″ × 87″ batting

Cutting

Star Blocks (25)

From a small print, cut one 3½″ × 42″ strip and one 2″ × 42″ strip. Cut into nine 3½″ squares (A, E) and eight 2″ squares (B). Repeat until you have enough matching sets for 25 blocks.

From the black, cut fourteen 2″ × 42″ strips. Cut into one hundred 2″ × 3½″ rectangles (C) and one hundred 2″ squares (D). Cut twenty-five 3½″ × 42″ strips. Cut into one hundred 3½″ × 6½″ rectangles (F) and one hundred 3½″ squares (G).

Sashing

From the black, cut twenty-two 2½″ × 42″ strips. Cut into two 2½″ × 16½″ strips (A), twelve 2½″ × 14½″ strips (B), and fifty 2½″ × 12½″ strips (C).

From a small print, cut one 2½″ square (D) for the sashing square/ small star center and eight 1½″ squares (E) for the small star points. Repeat until you have enough matching sets for 24 small stars.

Setting Triangles

From the black, cut three 21¼″ squares; cut diagonally in both directions for 12 setting triangles. Cut two 12″ squares; cut diagonally in half for four corner triangles.

Making the Blocks

1. Stitch two matching B squares to each C rectangle to make 100 Flying Geese units.

2. Join pieces A, B, C, and D to make twenty-five 6″ Sawtooth Star blocks.

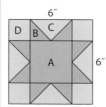

Sawtooth Star block
Make 25.

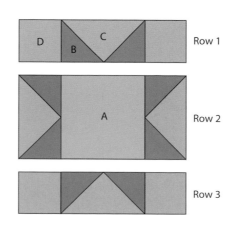

3. Stitch 2 E squares to each F rectangle to make 100 Flying Geese units. Join the 6″ Sawtooth Star blocks and pieces E, F and G to make twenty-five 12″ Double Sawtooth Star blocks.

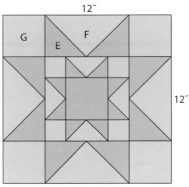

Double Sawtooth Star block
Make 25.

Putting the Quilt Top Together

1. Lay out the blocks in diagonal rows. Insert sashing strips A, B, and C; sashing squares D; and the setting triangles as shown in the quilt diagram on the right. Adjust your arrangement as needed so that the star colors move around the quilt.

2. Stitch two 1½″ squares to the ends of the sashing strips, as if you were making Flying Geese units. Match the colors to the sashing squares. When the sashing strips and squares are joined, these pieces will form small stars.

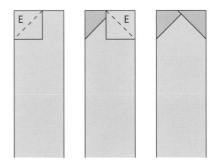

Making the Small Star Points

3. Stitch the blocks, sashing strips, and setting triangles together in diagonal rows. Press toward the sashing. Stitch the remaining sashing strips and sashing squares

together. Press. Join the block rows and sashing rows together. Press. Add the corner triangles. Press. Note that the setting triangles are slightly larger than required. Use your rotary cutter and ruler to true up the edges.

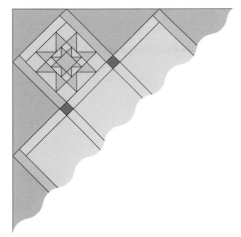

Trim the edges as needed

Quilting and Finishing

Refer to pages 106–108 for quilting and finishing instructions.

1. Layer and baste the quilt. Quilt by hand or machine. The stars in Primarily Stars are outline-quilted and then quilted again ¼″ in from the edge. A simple, traditional quilting design is used in the setting triangles.

2. Finish the quilt.

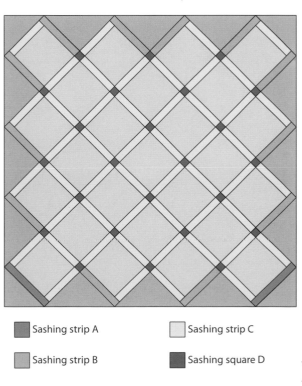

■ Sashing strip A

□ Sashing strip C

■ Sashing strip B

■ Sashing square D

New York Beauty Quilt

New York Beauty Quilt, 39″ x 39″, made by Alex Anderson and Gloria Smith

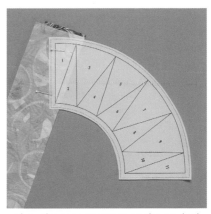

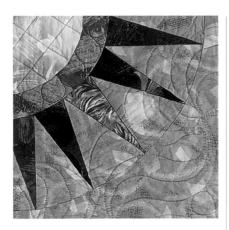

Gloria Smith did an excellent job working with my first line of fabrics with P&B Textiles. Paper piecing the spikey arcs results in perfect points. Use the darkest colors for the spikes to make them really stand out.

Materials

Yardage is based on 42˝-wide fabric.

Purples: ½ yard for spikes

Blues and teals: 1⅔ yards for spikes

Reds and pinks: 1⅔ yards for spikes

Orange: ⅓ yard for inner arcs

Yellow: ½ yard for centers

Yellow: 2½ yards for background

Backing: 1¼ yards

Batting: 43˝ × 43˝

Binding: ⅓ yard

Cutting

You will need 16 blocks.

Rough Cut: (for each block)

Background: Cut one 3˝ strip.

Spikes: Cut one 2½˝ × 4½˝ rectangle from each fabric (20 total).

Making the Block

1. Cut out the arc pattern (page 80) on the dashed line.

2. Place a background strip (#1) and a spike rectangle (#2), right sides together, with the strip on top.

3. Place the paper pattern, *printed side up*, on top of the fabric. Be sure the edges of the fabric extend at least ¼˝ past the lines on the paper pattern. Pin.

4. Stitch along the stitching line between 1 and 2.

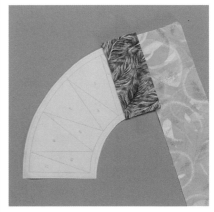

Place the paper pattern on the stacked fabrics and stitch.

5. Turn the paper pattern over and fold on the stitched line and trim the seam allowance to ¼˝.

6. Press open.

Press.

7. Turn the paper pattern over and fold the paper on the line between 2 and 3.

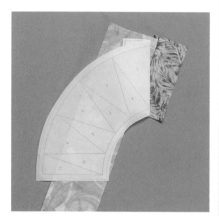

Fold.

8. Trim the seam allowance to ¼˝.

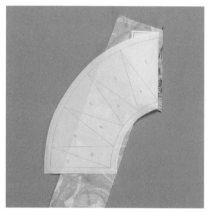

Trim.

9. Trim off the extra background strip length.

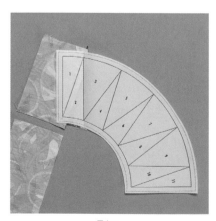

Trim.

10. Turn the paper pattern over and place a background strip (#3) on top of the spike fabric, with right sides together, matching the raw edge with the edge that was just trimmed. Pin.

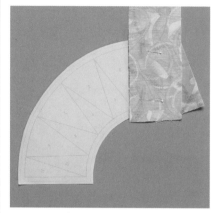

Place a strip and pin.

11. Turn the paper pattern over and stitch along the stitching line between 2 and 3.

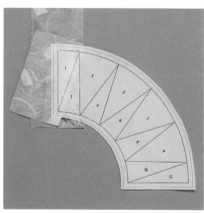

Stitch.

12. Turn the paper pattern over and press open.

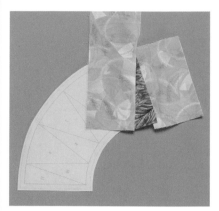

Press.

13. Turn the paper pattern over and fold the paper on the line between 3 and 4, and trim the seam allowance to ¼˝. Trim off the excess strip.

Fold and trim.

14. Turn the paper pattern over and place a spike rectangle (#4) on top of the background piece, with right sides together, matching the raw edge with the edge that was just trimmed. Pin.

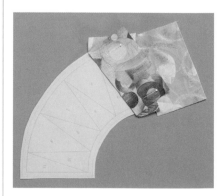

Pin.

15. Turn the paper pattern over and stitch along the line between 3 and 4.

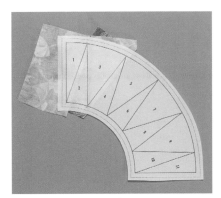

Stitch.

16. Repeat from Step 6, adding background strips and spike rectangles to complete the arc.

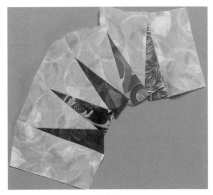

Add.

17. Place the pieced arc with the paper pattern on top, and trim on the dashed line.

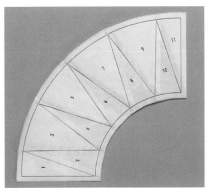

Trim on the dashed line.

Block Construction

1. Trace patterns A, B, and C (pages 80–81) onto the dull side of the freezer paper and cut out on the dashed line. Press A onto the background fabric, B onto inner arc fabric, and C onto center fabric.

2. Cut out A, B, and C on the dashed line. Your freezer paper template can be used up to six times.

Block pieces laid out.

3. Fold A in half and finger press to mark the center of the curved edge.

4. Match the center of the pieced arc and the center of the curved edge of A and pin. Then pin the two outside edges. Pin slightly away from the curved edge.

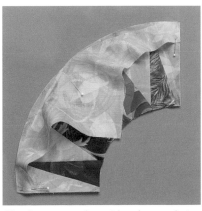

Match center and outside edges and pin.

5. Continue pinning the curve, aligning the raw edges.

Continue pinning.

6. Turn the paper pattern over and stitch along the solid ¼˝ sewing line. Press toward A.

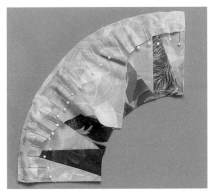

Stitch and press.

7. Remove the paper from the pieced arc.

8. Fold B in half and finger-press to mark the center of the longer curved edge.

9. Match the center of the pieced arc with the center of B and pin. Then pin the two outside edges as you did in Step 4.

Smaller arcs are a little trickier to maneuver than larger arcs. Clip the seam allowance of the convex curve (⅛˝ deep) to help ease the curve into position.

10. Continue pinning the curve, aligning the raw edges.

Continue pinning.

11. Stitch using ¼″ seam allowance with B on top. Press toward B.

Press.

12. Repeat Steps 8–11 to add piece C. Stitch with C on top. Press toward B.

Completed block

Putting the Quilt Top Together

Press following the arrows.

1. Arrange your blocks as shown on page 79 in a straight set.

2. Sew the blocks into rows. Press.

3. Sew the rows together. Press.

BORDERS

Paper piece 16 of the 3½″ × 8″ spiked border units using the same procedure as for the arcs. Sew four units together to create one border. Make a total of four borders (one for each edge of the quilt). You will paper piece these as you did the arcs. Do NOT remove the paper yet.

Border Corners

1. Trace C and D onto the dull side of the freezer paper and cut out on the dashed line. Press C onto the background fabric and D onto inner arc fabric.

2. Cut out C and D on the dashed line. Remove the freezer paper. Your freezer paper template can probably be used for all four corners.

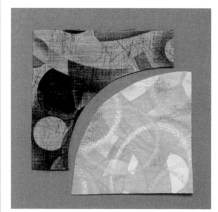

Block pieces laid out.

3. Fold C in half and finger-press to mark the center of the curved edge.

4. Match the center of the arc and the center of the curved edge of C and pin. Then pin the two outside edges. Continue pinning the curve, aligning the raw edges.

Match center and outside edges and pin.

5. Sew and press toward D.

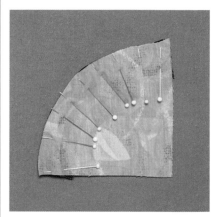

Stitch.

Attaching the Borders

1. Sew the top and bottom borders onto the quilt. Press toward the quilt top.

2. Sew the corners onto the two side borders.

3. Sew the side borders on and press toward the quilt top.

4. Carefully remove the paper.

Quilting and Finishing

Refer to pages 106–108 for quilting and finishing instructions.

1. Layer and baste the quilt. Quilt by hand or machine.

2. Finish the quilt.

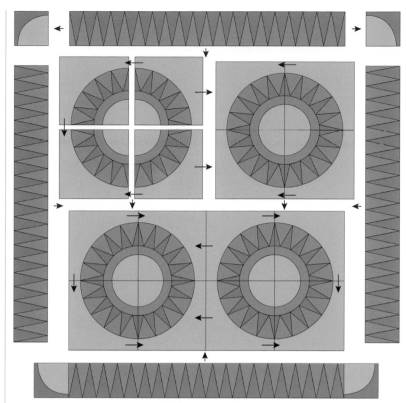

Quilt construction

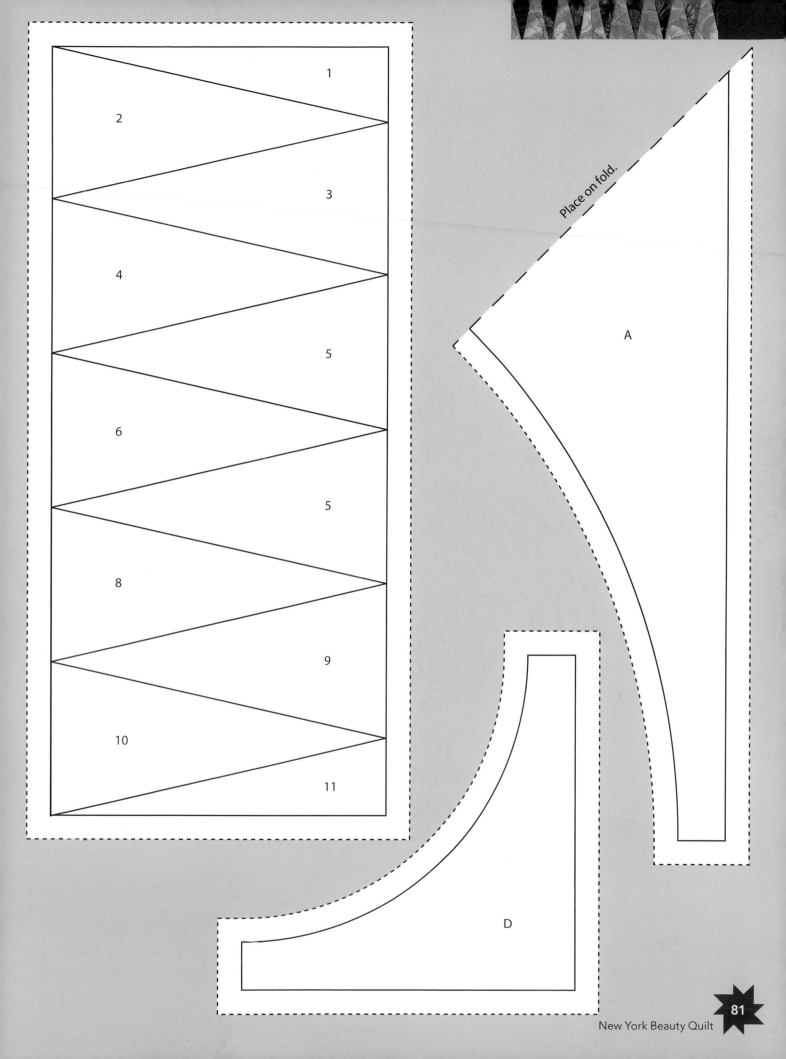

1

2

3

4

5

6

5

8

9

10

11

Place on fold.

A

D

radiant beauty

Radiant Beauty, 70˝ × 70˝, made by Valori Wells

Radiant Beauty introduces an irregular New York Beauty block. The points are varied in size and overlap at random, creating playful movement. To make the piecing match at each side, the block is flipped over and joined to its mirror image. This is the first irregular block I drafted, and I found the process unexpectedly gratifying. The other fun part of this quilt is the extra-wide border—a full eight strips deep—with mitered corners. The added color bands frame the quilt and help contain the exuberant arcs that seem to spin within.

Materials

Yardage is based on 42″-wide fabric.

Blocks:

1½ yards green frog print

1¼ yards muted green

⅔ yard green/brown print

⅝ yard each two different purples

½ yard yellow

Scraps (12″ × 12″):

four assorted red/pink prints

four assorted green prints

four assorted red/pink/purple prints

one gold/tan print

one orange print

one yellow print

Borders:

1¼ yards purple

⅔ yard multi pink/gold

⅔ yard red

⅜ yard light gold

⅜ yard pink

⅜ yard medium gold

⅜ yard multi pink/purple

⅜ yard rust

Also:

½ yard black for binding

4¼ yards backing

74″ × 74″ batting

Cutting

RADIANT BEAUTY BLOCKS (16)

Use the patterns on pages 89–96. Join sections B1 and B2, Br1 and Br2, A1 and A2, and Ar1 and Ar2 as indicated on the patterns. Prepare 8 B and 8 Br paper-piecing patterns. Prepare freezer paper patterns A, Ar, C, Cr, D, Dr, E, and Er.

From the green frog print, cut 8 A and 8 Ar.

From the muted green and the green/brown print, cut sixteen 3¾″ × 42″ strips total for B and Br.

From the two purples, cut twelve 3″ × 42″ strips total for B and Br.

From the yellow, cut four 3″ × 42″ strips total for B and Br.

From two red/pink prints, cut 2 C and 1 Cr. From the other two red/pink prints, cut 1 C and 2 Cr.

From two green prints, cut 2 D and 1 Dr. From the other two green prints, cut 1 D and 2 Dr.

From two red/purple/pink prints, cut 2 E and 1 Er. From the other two red/purple/pink prints, cut 1 E and 2 Er.

From the gold/tan print, cut 2 C and 2 Cr.

From the orange print, cut 2 D and 2 Dr.

From the yellow print, cut 2 E and 2 Er.

Sort the pieces by block, matching the colors.

BORDERS

From each border fabric, cut eight 42″-long strips at the widths listed below. Sew into eight long strips, one per color. Cut into the following border strips:

four 1½″ × 75″ light gold (A)	four 2½″ × 75″ red (E)
four 1½″ × 75″ pink (B)	four 1½″ × 75″ multi pink/purple (F)
four 2½″ × 75″ multi pink/gold (C)	four 1½″ × 75″ rust (G)
four 1½″ × 75″ medium gold (D)	four 4½″ × 75″ purple (H)

PAPER-PIECING IRREGULAR POINTS

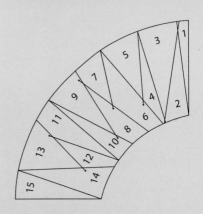

On a paper-piecing pattern for an irregular arc, the stitching lines do not always extend to the bottom or top edge. The idea is to allow the points to overlap and intersect without excess fabric buildup. Here's how to sew the arc:

1. Place the two contrasting B strips right sides together, with the background fabric on top and the point fabric underneath, just as you would for a symmetrical arc (see Block Construction on page 75–77). Place pattern B on top, marked side up, so that section 1 rests on top of the fabrics and the stitching line between sections 1 and 2 falls ¼″ from the edge of the strips. Pin if desired.

2. Stitch on the line exactly as it is marked on the pattern. If the stitching line stops just beyond the intersection of two lines, start or end your stitching at that point too.

3. Trim the background fabric only even with the edge of the paper pattern. Turn the work over, flip back the point fabric, and finger-press the seam, just as you would for a symmetrical arc.

4. Turn the work pattern side up. Fold back and crease the paper pattern on the stitching line that borders section 3. Let the paper tear a bit, if necessary, to accommodate the two or three stitches that cross over the stitching line.

5. Using scissors or a rotary cutter, trim the point fabric ¼″ beyond the folded edge. Unfold the pattern and trim off the excess point fabric even with the pattern edge.

6. Refold the pattern on the crease. Lay the background strip right side up. Place the work on top, pattern side up, and align the raw edges of the point fabric and the background strip. Unfold the pattern, marked side up. Stitch on the line. Some stitching lines extend across the width of the arc and others are shorter. Follow the paper pattern.

7. Turn the work pattern side down. Flip the background fabric over the ¼″ seam allowance to reveal the first point. Finger-press the seam.

8. Repeat steps 4–7, alternating between the two fabrics and following the numbered order on the pattern, until the entire arc is pieced. Press on the right side. Trim the excess fabric even with the pattern edge. Tear off and discard the paper pattern.

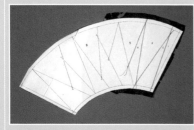

Two points are stitched

A view of the right side

Making the Blocks

1. Refer to pages 75–77 for guidance in piecing the arcs and Paper-Piecing Irregular Points (page 84). Make 6 B and 6 Br arcs with purple points and muted green and green/brown backgrounds. Make 2 B and 2 Br arcs with yellow points and green/brown backgrounds. Try to vary the fabric coloration from point to point, as shown in the quilt photograph (page 82).

2. Refer to pages 77–78 to sew the C, D, and E and the Cr, Dr, and Er pieces together. Use the red/pink, green, and red/purple/pink prints to make 4 sets of 3, or 12 total (6 in reverse). Use the gold/tan, orange, and yellow prints to make 4 total (2 in reverse).

3. Sew the A, B, and CDE units together. Make 12 red/green/purple blocks (reverse 6) and 4 yellow/green blocks (reverse 2).

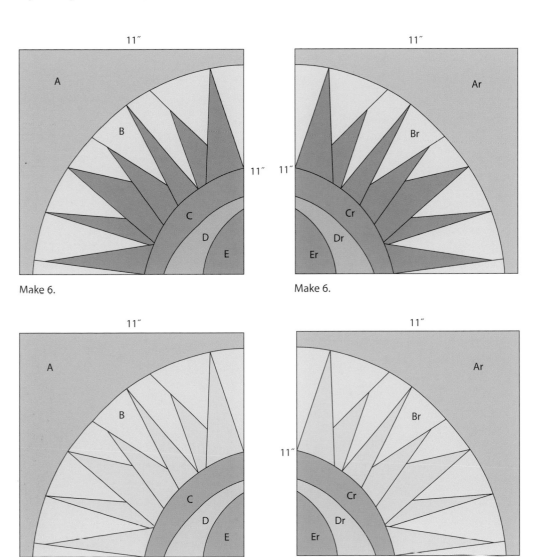

Make 6.

Make 6.

Make 2.

Make 2.

Radiant Beauty Blocks

Radiant Beauty Blocks

Putting the Quilt Top Together

1. Lay out the blocks in 4 rows of 4 blocks each, placing the arcs and colors as shown in the quilt photograph (page 82) and quilt diagram. Stitch the blocks together in rows. Press. Join the rows. Press.

2. Lay out border strips A through H side by side in order. Stitch A and B together along the long edges. Press toward B. Stitch C to AB. Press toward C. Continue adding the strips in order, pressing after each addition. Make 4 borders total, each 13½˝ × 75˝. Refer to Mitered Corners Borders (pages 104–105) to attach and complete the borders.

Block Key

- Radiant Beauty block
- Radiant Beauty reverse block
- Radiant Beauty block
- Radiant Beauty reverse block

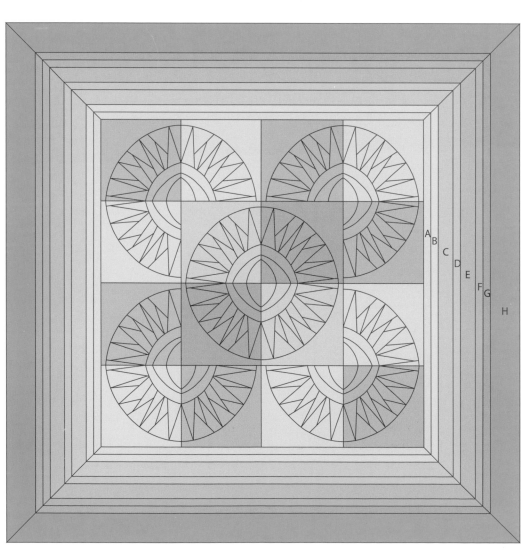

Quilt Diagram

Quilting and Finishing

Refer to pages 106–108 for quilting and finishing instructions.

1. Layer and baste the quilt. Quilt by hand or machine.

For this quilt, I let the fabric patterns and piecing seam lines influence my quilting direction. I quilted points in the centers of the New York Beauty blocks and wavy lines in the pieced points. I laid out the quilt and drew mini New York Beauty half-blocks at random in the border and quilted them with purple thread. For the rest of the background and border, I borrowed the leaf outline from the frog fabric, quilting in a continuous line and adding swirly tendrils. This leaf stitching filled in nicely without taking away from the designs in the fabric. I always strive to quilt in a complementary way, to bring the quilt to a satisfying conclusion, but without rushing or hurrying the process.

2. Finish the quilt.

Radiant Beauty quilting design
Enlarge as desired.

Attach to Ar1 here.

Radiant Beauty Block
Ar2

Cr

Radiant Beauty Block

Radiant
Beauty
Block

Dr

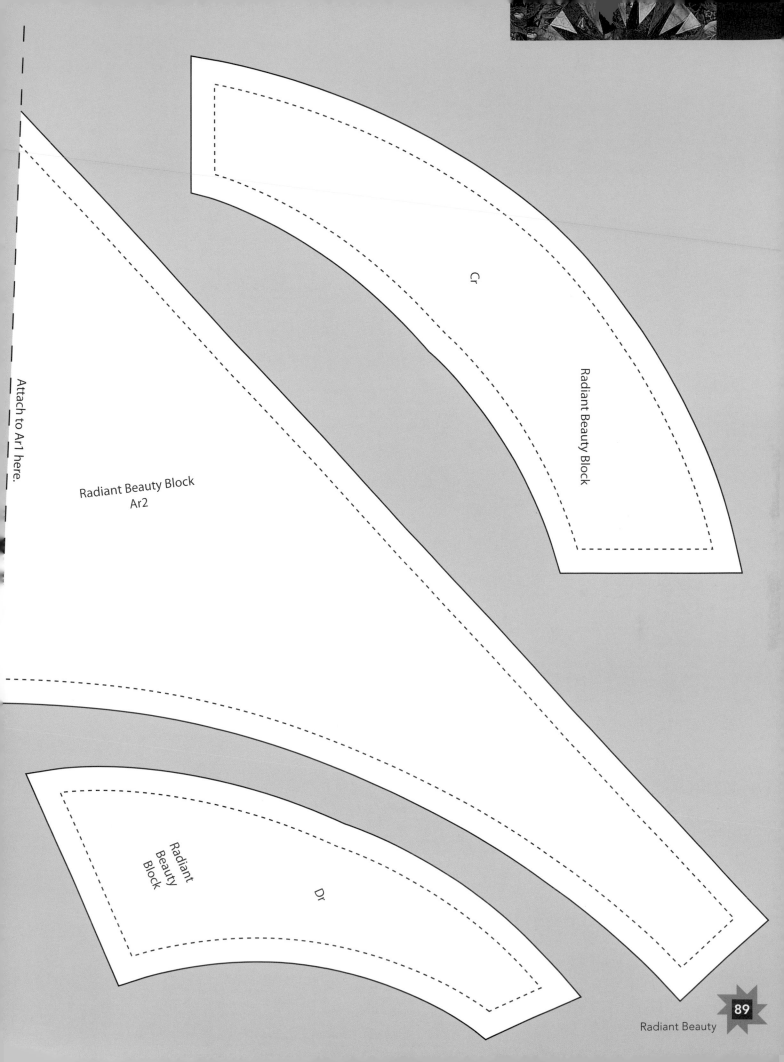

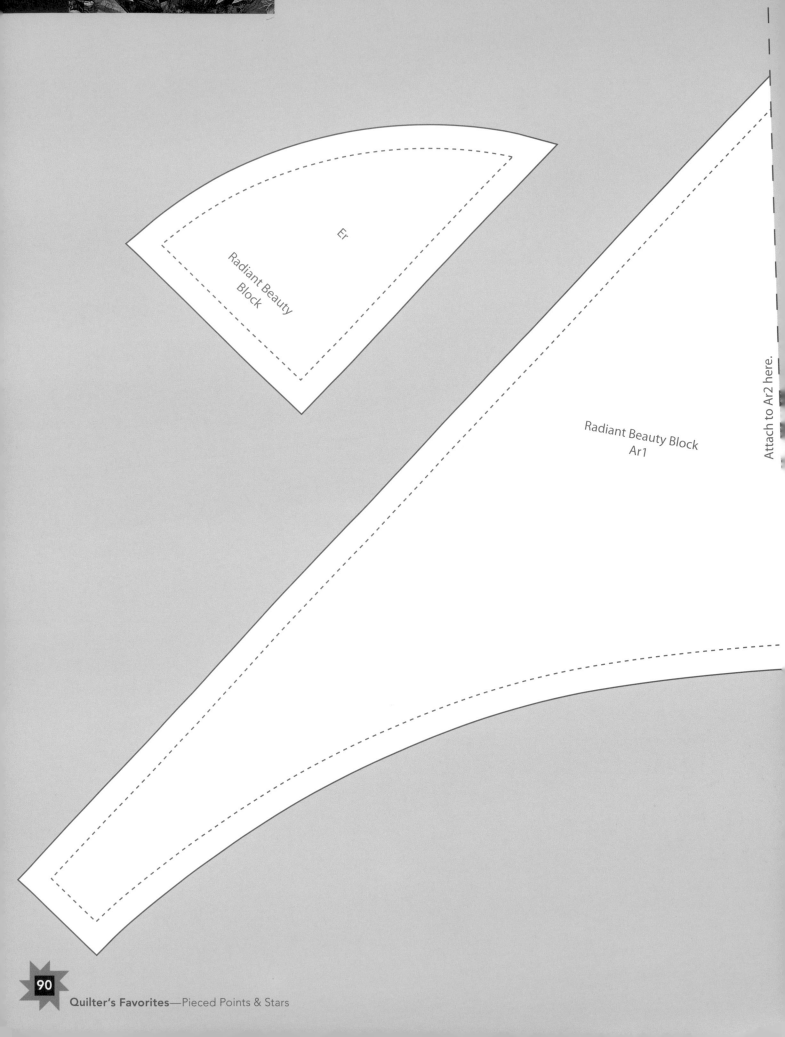

Er

Radiant Beauty
Block

Radiant Beauty Block
Ar1

Attach to Ar2 here.

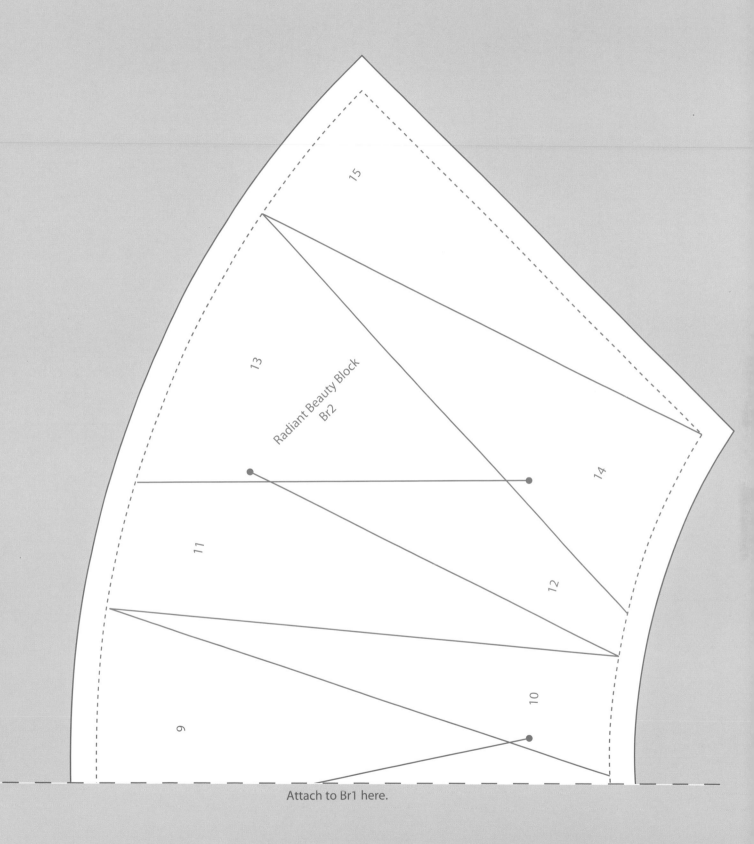

15

13

Radiant Beauty Block
Br2

14

11

12

9

10

Attach to Br1 here.

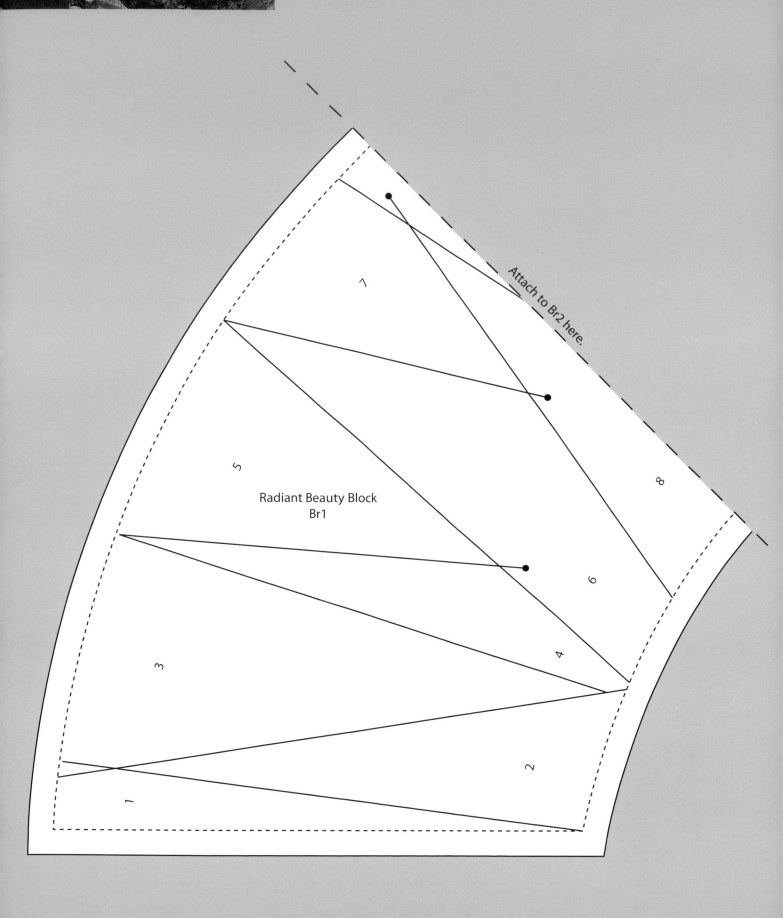

Radiant Beauty Block
Br1

Attach to Br2 here.

1
2
3
4
5
6
7
8

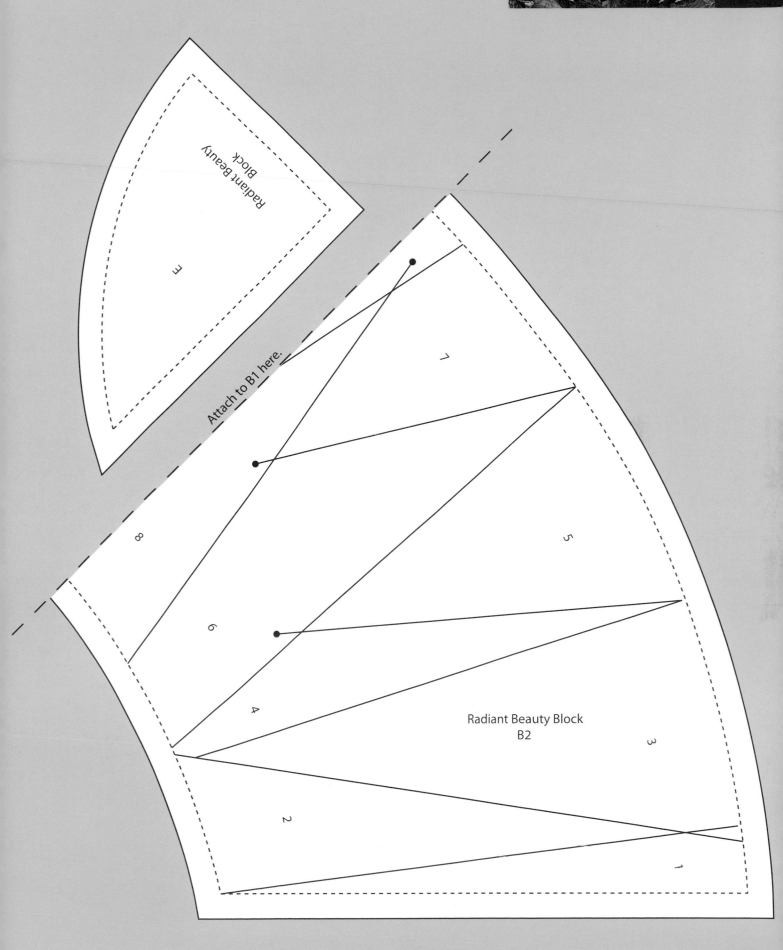

Radiant Beauty
Block

E

Attach to B1 here.

8

6

4

2

7

5

Radiant Beauty Block
B2

3

1

Radiant Beauty Block

C

Radiant Beauty Block
A1

Attach to A2 here.

Radiant
Beauty
Block

D

Radiant Beauty Block
A2

Attach to A1 here.

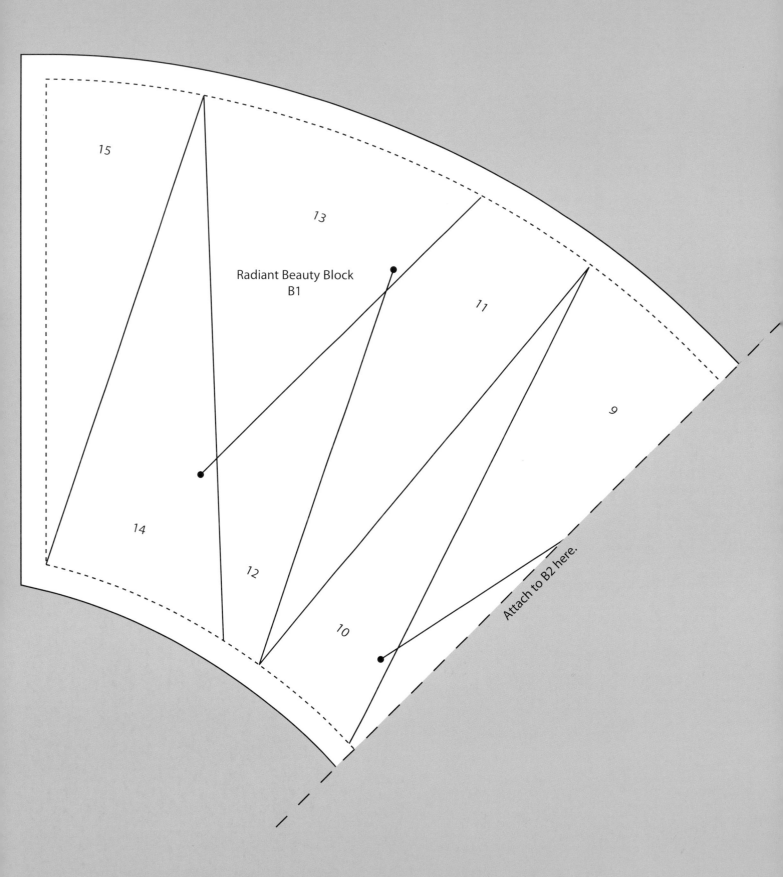

15

13

Radiant Beauty Block
B1

11

9

14

12

10

Attach to B2 here.

QUILTING basics

General Guidelines

SEAM ALLOWANCES

A ¼˝ seam allowance is used for most projects. It's a good idea to do a test seam before you begin sewing to check that your ¼˝ is accurate. Accuracy is the key to successful piecing.

PRESSING

In general, press seams toward the darker fabric. Press lightly in an up-and-down motion. Avoid using a very hot iron or over-ironing, which can distort shapes and blocks.

Paper Piecing

Once you get used to it, paper piecing is an easy way to ensure that your blocks will be accurate. You sew on the side of the paper with the printed lines. Fabric is placed on the non-printed side.

1. Trace or photocopy the number of paper-piecing patterns needed for your project.

2. Use a smaller-than-usual stitch length (1.5–1.8 or 18 to 20 stitches per inch), and a slightly larger needle (size 90/14). This makes the paper removal easier, and will result in tighter stitches that can't be pulled apart when you tear the paper off.

3. Cut the pieces slightly larger than necessary—about ¾˝ larger; they do not need to be perfect shapes. (One of the joys of paper piecing!)

With paper piecing you don't have to worry about the grain of the fabric. You are stitching on paper and that stabilizes the block. The paper is not torn off until after the blocks are stitched together.

4. Follow the number sequence when piecing. Pin piece #1 in place on the blank side of the paper, but make sure you don't place the pin anywhere near a seam line. Hold the paper up to the light to make sure the piece covers the area it is supposed to, with the seam allowance also amply covered.

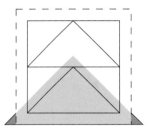

5. Fold the pattern back at the stitching line and trim the fabric to a ¼˝ seam allowance with a ruler and rotary cutter.

6. Cut piece #2 large enough to cover the area of #2 plus a generous seam allowance. It's a good idea to cut each piece larger than you think necessary; it might be a bit wasteful, but it's easier than ripping out tiny stitches! Align the edge with the trimmed seam allowance of piece #1, right sides together, and pin. Paper side up, stitch one line.

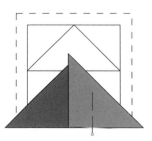

7. Open piece #2 and press.

8. Continue stitching each piece in order, being sure to fold back the paper pattern and trim the seam allowance to ¼" before adding the next piece.

9. Trim all around the finished unit to the ¼" seam allowance. Leave the paper intact until after the blocks have been sewn together, then carefully remove it. Creasing the paper at the seam line helps when tearing it.

Folded Piping

Amish Baskets (page 29) features a narrow, folded piping (no cording inside) inserted between its outermost border and mitered binding. This accent acts like a double mat on a nicely framed picture, adding a flash of color and a touch of elegance.

To figure how wide to cut the piping, multiply the desired finished width of the piping by 2, and add ½" for seam allowances.

For quilts with straight sides, cut piping strips from the straight grain of the fabric. For quilts with curved edges, cut strips on the bias. You can cut strips on the bias for design purposes as well.

1. Prepare the quilt for binding by trimming the batting and backing ⅛" beyond the raw edge of the quilt top.

2. Measure the quilt through the center, both horizontally and vertically. Add 2"–3" to both the length and width, and cut 2 strips to each measurement, piecing them if necessary. Press the seams open. Fold the strips lengthwise, right side out, and press.

3. Pin the piping strips to the appropriate sides of the quilt, aligning the raw edges with the raw edges of the quilt top. The strips should overlap and extend beyond each corner by 1"–1½". Baste the strips to the quilt with a ⅛" seam.

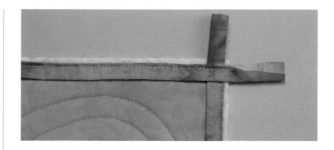

4. Align the raw edge of the binding with the raw edge of the piping and quilt top. Stitch the binding to the quilt with your chosen technique. Trim the excess ends of the piping strips.

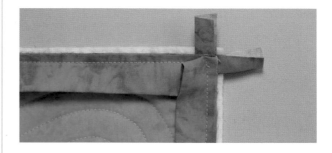

5. Turn the binding to the quilt back and finish. Turn your quilt over and admire your piping!

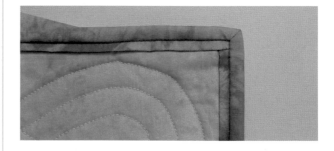

If your quilt features piecing in the outermost border (e.g., the Cake Stand corner blocks in Amish Baskets), you may need to make slight adjustments so the piping doesn't cover any points. Before trimming the backing and batting, position the piping as you wish it to appear on the finished quilt. Baste the piping in place, and trim the batting and backing to the piping's raw edge. (For *Amish Baskets*, the batting and backing were trimmed approximately ⅛" beyond the quilt top.) Align the binding with the raw edges of the piping, batting, and backing, and stitch with a generous ¼" seam.

Making Y Blocks

Y block

There are many methods for making the Y block. But, you should be warned: *the standard line-drawing technique does not yield the results you need.* That technique gives you two mirror-image blocks, and what you need are identical blocks.

Each triangle is assigned a number, so keep the 1, 2, 3 in your head and sew a ¼˝ seam allowance.

KEEPING TRACK OF FABRIC POSITIONS

When you need to figure out where a fabric goes in a block, orient the block so it looks like a lowercase letter Y. Position 1 is the quarter-square triangle on the lower left side. Position 2 is the quarter-square triangle on top, and Position 3 is the half-square triangle on the lower right side.

Use this diagram as a guide for creating your Y blocks.

In the Block Construction charts, you will see blank block diagrams that you can use when planning your projects. Draw a matching sketch large enough that you can glue small scraps of fabric in their proper positions. This will help you remember the right fabric position when it is time to cut or sew. Be sure to label your sketch so you know which end is the top.

POSITIONS 1 & 2: THE ¼ SQUARE TRIANGLES

1. Cut a square each of Position 1 and Position 2 fabric that is 1½˝ larger than the *finished* block. For every pair of Position 1 and Position 2 squares you cut, you have enough quarter-square triangles to make 4 completed Y blocks when the Position 3 fabric is added.

2. Place the Position 1 and Position 2 fabrics right sides together on the cutting mat. The Position 2 fabric goes on the bottom and the Position 1 fabric on top. If you have done this correctly you will be looking at the wrong side of the Position 1 fabric when you go to make your cut. Cut this stack twice diagonally from corner to corner.

Position 1 fabric is always on top when you are making the crosscut.

3. Keeping the Position 1 fabric on top, stack the pairs of triangles so that the right angle (the 90° angle) points to the upper right. This square edge is easier to feed under the presser foot. Stacking the triangles this way by your sewing machine means everything is positioned correctly to start your chain stitching.

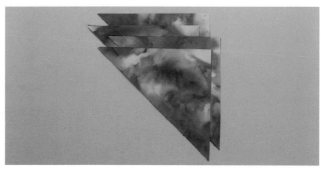

Position the triangle pairs just like this.

4. Chain stitch the triangles together along the right edge using a ¼˝ seam allowance.

Chain stitching

5. Press toward the Position 2 fabric.

Pressing the chain-stitched work

ADDING THE POSITION 3 TRIANGLE

1. Cut 2 squares of the Position 3 fabric 1˝ larger than the finished square. Cut the squares once diagonally from corner to corner. Two squares of the Position 3 fabric will complete four Y blocks when added to the Position 1 and Position 2 units.

> ### tip
>
> Don't trim these yet! This Position 1 and 2 unit is intentionally larger than the Position 3 triangle so you can align the long bias edge and still be able to line up the opposing point of the Position 3 triangle with the seam allowance of the pieced triangle.

2. Place these half-squares right sides together on top of the half-squares you made from the Position 1 and Position 2 fabrics. Make sure the diagonal edges are even and match the right-angle points.

Align the Position 3 half-squares with the Position 1 and 2 half-squares, right sides together.

3. Chain stitch the blocks together along the diagonal edge.

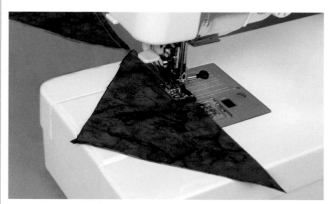

Chain stitch the units together.

SQUARING UP

Before pressing the block open, square the block to 5½˝ × 5½˝ for *Pyramid Color Play* and 6½˝ × 6½˝ for *Triangles All Around*.

1. Place your square ruler on a flat surface with the underside facing up. Put some tape just to the left side of the printed diagonal line, so when you align the seam between the 2 small triangles you can see that the line is directly on top of the stitching.

2. Draw a line joining the measurement of the unfinished blocks on the ruler. In the photo below that is 5½″. This line should be perpendicular to the diagonal line and form the outlines of Position 1 and Position 2 on the ruler. Place a second piece of tape along this line. Make sure the tape is just above the marked line, not on top of it. *This ruler should now give you perfect squares every time.*

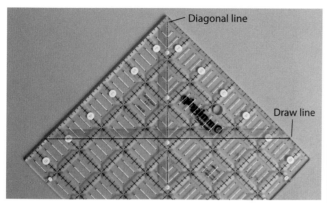

Marking the ruler

3. Before the square is pressed at the long seam allowance, square it to the unfinished size. Check the first few blocks as they are cut to see if your tape is placed correctly. The diagonal seams should come right to the corners of the unfinished squares. Adjust if necessary.

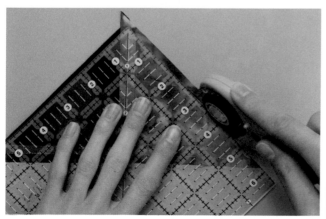

Squaring up

4. Press toward the large Position 3 triangle and trim the dog-ears.

Stacking blocks

Trimming dog-ears

Using Templates

First, press your fabric right sides together. Place the template on the fabric, aligning the indicated grain lines to the grain of your fabric and trace with a sharp marking device—a mechanical pencil with a soft lead, or whatever shows up on the fabric, with a point sharp enough to mark right next to the edge of the template. Butt the template up to previously drawn lines and continue until you have the number of pieces you need.

Then cut. Your goal is to cut fabric pieces the same size as the templates—neither bigger nor smaller. Cutting doubled fabric speeds the process: you get two pieces for each one traced, and many of the pieces are reversing shapes.

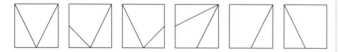

Most of the time you may need both right-facing and left-facing pieces, as noted in the instructions. By cutting double, you automatically get rights and lefts. Special note is made if the template must be used on a single layer of fabric, cut one way only.

ROTARY CUTTING TEMPLATE PIECES

If you need many of the same shape from the same fabric, cut a strip of fabric the height of the template.

Cut height of template

Use your template to mark the other lines.

Then, use a small acrylic ruler and cutter to cut on the pencil lines.

If you are making a smaller quilt and only need, for example, eight Gs, four As, and two Js, trace around the templates as you would for scissors cutting.

But, instead of using scissors, use an acrylic ruler to cut pieces free from a larger piece of fabric, then cut on the pencil lines.

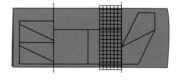

This way you can maintain accuracy while working with the tool with which you feel more comfortable. When you have cut enough pieces to see what you have, go on to the next step.

All-Star Lineup

The challenge with star making is working with several different shapes that often appear not to fit together. If your cutting has been handled correctly, it's just a matter of learning how the shapes fit together. The All-Star Lineup gives you a pictorial guide of how to align odd shapes that will be sewn together.

4

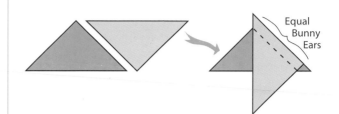

Equal Bunny Ears

1

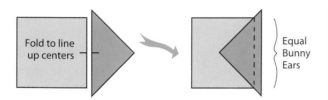

Fold to line up centers

Equal Bunny Ears

5

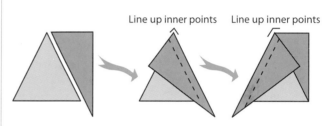

Line up inner points   Line up inner points

2

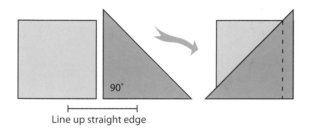

90°

Line up straight edge

6

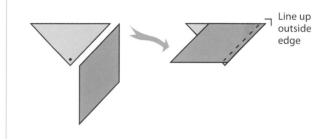

Line up outside edge

3

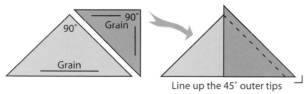

90°   90°
Grain
Grain

Line up the 45° outer tips

7

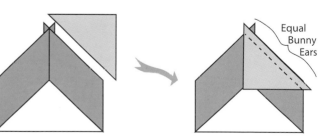

Equal Bunny Ears

After you have pieced your shapes together and are confident you have resolved their pairing successfully, it's time to trim off the bunny ears. If something looks off, do not trim. With the "ears" still intact, you can remeasure to make sure the initial cut was correct.

Once you have assembled the individual units, which when combined will complete your star, it is time to sew them together. I find it helpful to lay out the block before assembling the units.

Look carefully where the tips intersect. It is important they occur ¼″ in from the unfinished edge.

¼ ″ in from unfinished edge

When sewing the units together, if one of the sections has a ¼″ intersection, always place it on top. You want to see where the intersection is occurring. Sew one hair to the right-hand side of the intersection. This allows for pressing. If the intersection has to be on the bottom, and you cannot see it, mark the point with a pin.

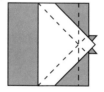

Borders

When border strips are to be cut on the crosswise grain, diagonally piece the strips together to achieve the needed lengths.

BUTTED BORDERS

In most cases the side borders are sewn on first. When you have finished the quilt top, measure it through the center vertically. This will be the length to cut the side borders. Place pins at the centers of all four sides of the quilt top, as well as in the center of each side border strip. Pin the side borders to the quilt top first, matching the center pins. Using a ¼″ seam allowance, sew the borders to the quilt top and press toward the border.

Measure horizontally across the center of the quilt top, including the side borders. This will be the length to cut the top and bottom borders. Repeat, pinning, sewing, and pressing.

MITERED CORNER BORDERS

Measure the length of the quilt top and add twice the cut width of your border, plus 5″. This is the length you need to cut or piece the side borders.

Place pins at the centers of both side borders and all four sides of the quilt top. From the center pin, measure in both directions and mark half of the measured length of the quilt top on both side borders. Pin, matching the centers and the marked length of the side border to the edges of the quilt top. Stitch the strips to the sides of the quilt top by starting ¼″ in from the beginning of the border seam, backstitching, and then continuing down the length of the side border. Stop stitching ¼″ before the edge of the quilt top, at the seam allowance line, and backstitch. The excess length of the side borders will extend beyond each edge. Press the seams toward the border.

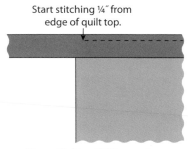

Start stitching ¼″ from edge of quilt top.

Stop stitching ¼″ from edge.

Determine the length needed for the top and bottom border the same way, measuring the width of the quilt top through the center including each side border. Add twice the cut width of your border plus 5″ to this measurement. Cut or piece these border strips to this length. From the center of each border strip, measure in both directions and mark half of the measured width of the quilt top. Again, pin, and then stitch up to the previous stitching line, and backstitch. The border strips extend beyond each end.

To create the miter, lay the corner on the ironing board. Working with the quilt right side up, lay one border strip on top of the adjacent border.

Press the top border seam allowance toward the border. With right sides up, fold the top border strip under itself so that it meets the edge of the adjacent border and forms a 45° angle. Pin the fold in place.

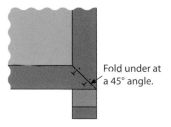

Fold under at a 45° angle.

Position a 90° angle triangle or ruler over the corner to check that the corner is flat and square. When everything is in place, press the fold firmly.

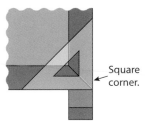

Square corner.

Remove the pins. Fold the center section of the top diagonally from the corner, right sides together, and align the long edges of the border strips. On the wrong side, place pins near the pressed fold in the corner to secure the border strips.

Beginning at the inside corner at the border seam line, stitch, backstitch, and then stitch along the fold toward the outside point of the border corners, being careful not to allow any stretching to occur. Backstitch at the end. Trim the excess border fabric to a ¼″ seam allowance. Press the seam open.

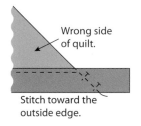

Wrong side of quilt.

Stitch toward the outside edge.

Backing

Plan on making the backing a minimum of 8″ longer and wider than the quilt top. Piece, if necessary. Trim the selvages before you piece to the desired size.

To economize, you can piece the back from any leftover quilting fabrics or blocks in your collection.

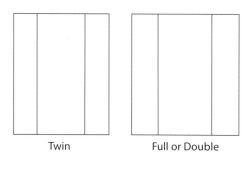

Twin   Full or Double

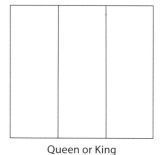

Queen or King

Batting

The type of batting to use is a personal decision; consult your local quilt shop. Cut batting approximately 8″ longer and wider than your quilt top.

Layering

Spread the backing wrong side up and tape the edges down with masking tape. (If you are working on carpet you can use T-pins to secure the backing to the carpet.) Center the batting on top, smoothing out any folds. Place the quilt top right side up on top of the batting and backing, making sure it is centered.

Basting

If you plan to machine quilt, pin baste the quilt layers together with safety pins placed a minimum of 3″–4″ apart. Begin basting in the center and move toward the edges first in vertical, then horizontal, rows.

If you plan to hand quilt, baste the layers together with thread using a long needle and light-colored thread. Knot one end of the thread. Using stitches approximately the length of the needle, begin in the center and move out toward the edges in vertical and horizontal rows approximately 4″ apart. Add 2 diagonal rows of basting.

Quilting

Quilting, whether by hand or machine, enhances the pieced or appliquéd design of the quilt. You may choose to quilt in-the-ditch, echo the pieced or appliqué motifs, use patterns from quilting design books and stencils, or do your own free-motion quilting. Suggested quilting patterns are included in some of the projects.

Binding

Trim excess batting and backing from the quilt.

DOUBLE FOLD STRAIGHT GRAIN BINDING (FRENCH FOLD)

If you want a ¼″ finished binding, cut the binding strips 2″ wide and piece together with diagonal seams to make a continuous binding strip. Press the seams open.

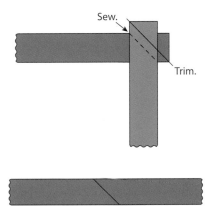

Press the entire strip in half lengthwise with wrong sides together. With raw edges even, pin the binding to the front edge of the quilt a few inches away from the corner, and leave the first few inches of the binding unattached. Start sewing, using a ¼″ seam allowance.

Stop ¼″ away from the first corner (see Step 1), and backstitch one stitch. Lift the presser foot and needle. Rotate the quilt one-quarter turn. Fold the binding at a right angle so it extends straight above the quilt and the fold forms a 45° angle in the corner (see Step 2). Then bring the binding strip down even with the edge of the quilt (see Step 3). Begin sewing at the folded edge. Repeat in the same manner at all corners.

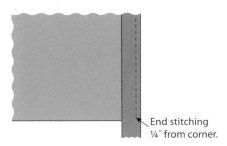

Step 1. Stitch to ¼" from corner.

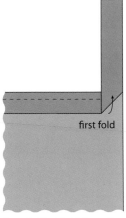

Step 2. First fold for miter

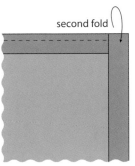

Step 3. Second fold alignment

Continue stitching until you are back near the beginning of the binding strip. See Finishing the Binding Ends for tips on finishing and hiding the raw edges of the ends of the binding.

CONTINUOUS BIAS BINDING

A continuous bias involves using a square sliced in half diagonally and then sewing the triangles together so that you continuously cut marked strips to make continuous bias binding. The same instructions can be used to cut bias for piping. Cut the fabric for the bias binding or piping so it is a square. For example, if yardage is ½ yard, cut an 18″ square. Cut the square in half diagonally, creating two triangles.

Sew these triangles together as shown, using a ¼˝ seam allowance. Press the seam open.

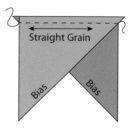

Using a ruler, mark the parallelogram with lines spaced the width you need to cut your bias. Cut along the first line about 5˝.

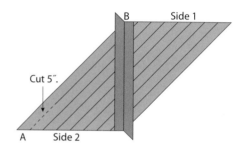

Join Side 1 and Side 2 to form a tube. Line A will line up with the raw edge at B. This will allow the first line to be offset by one strip width. Pin the raw ends together, making sure that the lines match. Sew with a ¼˝ seam allowance. Press the seam open. Cut along the drawn lines, creating one continuous strip.

Press the entire strip in half lengthwise with wrong sides together. Place the binding on the quilt as described in "Double Fold Straight Grain Binding (French Fold)" pages 107–108.

See Finishing the Binding Ends for tips on finishing and hiding the raw edges of the ends of the binding.

FINISHING THE BINDING ENDS

Method 1:

After stitching around the quilt, fold under the beginning tail of the binding strip ¼˝ so that the raw edge will be inside the binding after it is turned to the backside of the quilt. Place the end tail of the binding strip over the beginning folded end. Continue to attach the binding and stitch slightly beyond the starting stitches. Trim the excess binding. Fold the binding over the raw edges to the quilt back and hand stitch, mitering the corners.

Method 2:

Fold the ending tail of the binding back on itself where it meets the beginning binding tail. From the fold, measure and mark the cut width of your binding strip. Cut the ending binding tail to this measurement. For example, if your binding is cut 2¼˝ wide, measure from the fold on the ending tail of the binding 2¼˝ and cut the binding tail to this length.

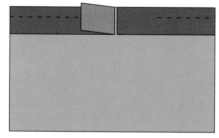

Fold, then cut binding tail to cut width of binding.

Open both tails. Place one tail on top of the other tail at right angles, right sides together. Mark a diagonal line and stitch on the line. Trim the seam to ¼˝. Press open.

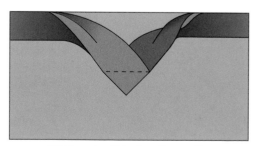

Stitch ends of binding diagonally.

Refold the binding and stitch this binding section in place on the quilt. Fold the binding over the raw edges to the quilt back and hand stitch, mitering the corners.

CONTRIBUTORS

Alex Anderson

Half-Square Triangle Quilt from
Kids Start Quilting with Alex Anderson

Star of Hope from *Rotary Cutting
with Alex Anderson*

Amish Baskets from *Finish It
with Alex Anderson*

Sun Ray from *Simply Stars*

New York Beauty Quilt from
Paper Piecing with Alex Anderson

Alex Anderson's love affair with quiltmaking began in 1978, when she completed her Grandmother's Flower Garden quilt as part of her work toward a degree in art at San Francisco State University. Over the years, her focus has rested on understanding fabric relationships and on an intense appreciation for traditional quilting surface design and star quilts.

Alex's mission is to educate, inspire, entertain, and grow today's quilting community. With this mission in mind, she has had the privilege and pleasure of ushering tens of thousands of new people into the world of quilting. For eleven years, she hosted television's premier quilt show, *Simply Quilts*, and she is currently the co-host and an executive producer of *The Quilt Show* with Ricky Tims (www.thequiltshow.com), an interactive website that features full production videos and is connecting quilters worldwide.

When Alex is not traveling, she resides in Northern California with her husband and kitty, and daily faces the challenges of feeding various forms of wildlife in her backyard.

Peggy Barkle

Curve-azy Stars from *Blendable Curves*

Peggy J. Barkle was born in Seattle, Washington, but grew up in the San Francisco Bay Area. She attended high school in San Francisco and studied interior design in college.

Peggy decided to leave the corporate world to stay home and raise twins, but soon she was looking for relief from the endless bottles, diapers, and dishes that came along with being a young wife and mother.

She loved her kids more than anything and wouldn't have traded a minute with them, but at the end of the day, she needed to be able to look at and touch something that defined her as a person and not just a wife and mother. By the time she ran across a PBS series on quilting hosted by Eleanor Burns, she had run through every craft known to man, but when she put fabric between her fingers, the search was over. She was hooked. She was home!

She began teaching in 1995 at a local quilt shop and area guilds. Her favorite students are the beginners, wide-eyed and eager. She has a room full of yardage and a brain full of ideas. She could not imagine doing anything else and considers being able to share what she loves an unbelievable blessing.

The kids are grown now, and fortunately so has Peggy's fabric stash.

Carol Doak

Sunrise from *Mariner's Compass Stars*

Hot, Hot, Hot! from *Mariner's Compass Stars*

Floral Stars from *Experts' Guide to
Foundation Piecing*

Carol Doak's passion for quiltmaking began in 1979, when she enrolled in a basic quilting class in Worthington, Ohio. She taught that class the following year and continues to share her passion with quilters worldwide through her sizable collection of best-selling books and popular classes. Her teaching style has been described as light-hearted and fun, and her goal is to inspire students in a positive way.

In 1994, her first paper-piecing book, *Easy Machine Paper Piecing*, popularized her trademark technique worldwide. Carol's impressive quilts have been featured on the covers of most national quilting magazines. Carol's book, *Carol Doak's Simply Sensational 9-Patch Stars*, offered quilters the opportunity to make over 2,500 paper-pieced nine-patch star block combinations.

In April 1999, Carol won the 8th Honors Award from the East Coast Quilters Alliance in recognition of her outstanding influence in the field of quilting. She has been named one of the top ten quilt teachers and designers in the United States, and in 2004 she was nominated as one of 24 All-American Quilters. In 2005, she was nominated as Professional Quilter of the Year. Carol resides in Windham, New Hampshire, with her husband.

M'Liss Rae Hawley

In the Limelight from *M'Liss Rae Hawley's Scrappy Quilts*

M'Liss Rae Hawley is an accomplished quilting teacher, lecturer, embroidery and textile designer, and a best-selling author. She conducts workshops and seminars throughout the world. As the author of many books and the originator of numerous innovative designs, M'Liss is constantly seeking new boundaries to challenge her students while imparting her enthusiasm and love for the art of quilting. She likes to break quilting down to the basics, in order to show students that quilting can be easy and fun at any level of skill!

M'Liss continues to create fabric with coordinating embroidery collections, write books, and create patterns for many magazines. M'Liss is also the spokesperson for several national and international companies

M'Liss and her husband, Michael, live on Whidbey Island, Washington, in a filbert orchard. Michael is also a best-selling author and the recently retired sheriff of Island County. Their son, Alexander, is a staff sergeant in the US Marine Corps, currently serving overseas, and their daughter, Adrienne, served in AmeriCorps, is a firefighter, and currently attends graduate school in Dublin, Ireland. Michael and M'Liss share their home with seven dachshunds and four cats.

Cheryl Malkowski

Pyramid Color Play from *Fun with One Block Quilts*

Triangles All Around from *Fun with One Block Quilts*

Cheryl Malkowski lives in Roseburg, Oregon, with her husband, Tom, and their dog, Bosco. She has two grown children and one grandchild, who is her favorite little boy.

She likes writing almost as much as teaching. She loves everything about the quilting process, especially the actual quilting, whether on a domestic machine or a longarm. Her quilting has been displayed at many shows, including the American Quilter's Society show in Paducah, Kentucky. Cheryl was a featured guest on *The Quilt Show* in the inaugural season, which is available on DVD from that site.

Linda Jenkins and Becky Goldsmith

Sun and Sea from *Piecing the Piece O' Cake Way*

The Green Country Quilter's Guild in Tulsa, Oklahoma, can be credited for brining Linda Jenkins and Becky Goldsmith together. Their friendship developed while they worked together on many guild projects and through a shared love for appliqué. This partnership led to the birth of Piece O' Cake Designs in 1994 and survived Linda's move to Pagosa Springs, Colorado, while Becky headed for Sherman, Texas.

Linda owned and managed a beauty salon before she started quilting. Over the years she developed a fine eye for color as a hair colorist and makeup artist. Becky's degree in interior design and many art classes provided a perfect background for quilting. Linda and Becky have shown many quilts and have won numerous awards. Together they make a dynamic quilting duo and love to teach other quilters the joys of appliqué.

In the fall of 2002 Linda and Becky joined the C&T Publishing family, where they continue to produce wonderful books and patterns.

Doreen Speckmann

Antigua from *Travels with Peaky & Spike*

Grand Cayman from *Travels with Peaky & Spike*

Playa del Carmen from *Travels with Peaky & Spike*

Doreen Speckmann was an accomplished quilt teacher, designer, and author who taught on quilting cruises and international quilting tours. Doreen passed away in 1999.

Jean Wells

Betsy's Baskets from *Patchwork Quilts Made Easy*

Primarily Stars from *Patchwork Quilts Made Easy*

Jean Wells has been an avid quilter for over thirty years, sharing her knowledge and ideas with thousands of quilters of all experience levels. A teacher at heart, she began sewing as a child, and her love of sewing led to a career as a home economics teacher and school counselor. About thirty years ago, she opened her quilt shop, The Stitchin' Post, in Sisters, Oregon, a small 1880s-style town at the foot of the Cascade mountains. The Stitchin' Post is one of the very first quilt shops opened in America and today is one of the premier shops featured in *American Patchwork & Quilting* magazine's "Quilt Shop Sampler."

Jean has written articles for magazines, lectured and taught quilting classes worldwide, conducted business classes for fellow quilt shop owners, and appeared on numerous television shows, including HGTV's *Simply Quilts*. Jean is a recipient of the Michael Kile Award for lifetime achievement in the quilting industry, and she was inducted into the Primedia Hall of Fame as one of the first "independent retailers" and also received her local community's "Business of the Year" award.

A love of gardening led Jean to open her second retail store, The Wild Hare, also in Sisters, where she offers unique garden-style accessories and decorative items. The combination of quilting and gardening has proved especially fruitful for Jean, and she often explores garden-related themes in her quiltmaking. In 2000, her quilt *Paradise in the Garden* won the Millennium Quilt Contest's Imagination Award. She used the cash prize to build a small greenhouse garden shed, which she has surrounded with flowers and vegetables.

Valori Wells

Radiant Beauty from *Radiant New York Beauties*

Valori Wells and her mother, Jean Wells, are a well-known duo involved in quiltmaking, fabric design, and operating The Stitchin' Post in Sisters, Oregon.

When Valori was in college, she and Jean began collaborating on quilting books with a garden flair. Valori's talents as a photographer captured nature at its best, and her inspirational images soon became the focus of her own distinctive quilting style. Her career came into full blossom when she began designing fabrics for the quilting industry. Valori returned to Sisters to join her mother in managing the store. Currently she is a designer for Free Spirit Textiles.

Valori has also been spreading her wings in the direction of soft furnishings and has teamed with Jean to create books on home furnishings.

Great Titles *from* C&T PUBLISHING

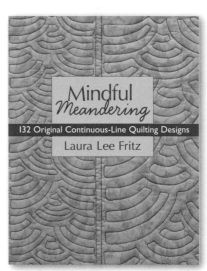

Available at your local retailer or **www.ctpub.com** *or* **800.284.1114**

For a list of other fine books from C&T Publishing, ask for a free catalog:

C&T PUBLISHING, INC.

P.O. Box 1456
Lafayette, CA 94549
800-284-1114

Email: ctinfo@ctpub.com
Website: www.ctpub.com

C&T Publishing's professional photography services are now available to the public. Visit us at www.ctmediaservices.com.

Tips and Techniques can be found at www.ctpub.com > Consumer Resources > Quiltmaking Basics: Tips & Techniques for Quiltmaking & More

For quilting supplies:

COTTON PATCH

1025 Brown Ave.
Lafayette, CA 94549
Store: 925-284-1177
Mail order: 925-283-7883

Email: CottonPa@aol.com
Website: www.quiltusa.com

Note: Fabrics used in the quilts shown may not be currently available, as fabric manufacturers keep most fabrics in print for only a short time.